Test Bank for
Structured FORTRAN 77 for Engineers and Scientists

third edition

Test Bank for
Structured FORTRAN 77
for Engineers and Scientists

third edition

D.M. ETTER
University of New Mexico, Albuquerque

Prepared with assistance from Mainuddin K. Murshed.

The Benjamin/Cummings Publishing Company, Inc.
Redwood City, California • Fort Collins, Colorado • Menlo Park, California
Reading, Massachusetts • New York • Don Mills, Ontario
Wokingham, U.K. • Amsterdam • Bonn • Sydney • Singapore • Tokyo
Madrid • San Juan

ISBN 0-8053-0053-8

ABCDEFGHIJ-AL-8932109

The Benjamin/Cummings Publishing Company, Inc.
390 Bridge Parkway
Redwood City, California 94065

PREFACE

Since quizzes and exams are such an important part of a university course, we have developed a separate supplement for these items to aid instructors using the third   Edition of STRUCTURED FORTRAN 77 FOR ENGINEERS AND SCIENTISTS. The items in this test bank are discussed below:

QUIZZES AND SOLUTIONS

Ten sets of quizzes, corresponding to the 10 chapters in the text, are included here. Each set contains 10, 15, or 20 quizzes, depending on the complexity of the chapter. Each quiz is printed on a separate page to allow simple copying of the quiz for classroom use. The solutions to all the quizzes are at the end of this section in a condensed format.

The chapter titles and the number of quizzes for the chapters is listed below:

Chapter 1	An introduction to FORTRAN 77 and Problem solving	10 quizzes
Chapter 2	Arithmetic Computations	15 quizzes
Chapter 3	Control Structures	20 quizzes
Chapter 4	Data files and More I/O	10 quizzes
Chapter 5	Array Processing	20 quizzes
Chapter 6	Implementing Top-Down Design with Functions	20 quizzes
Chapter 7	Implementing Top-Down Design with subroutines	20 quizzes
Chapter 8	Additional Data Types	15 quizzes
Chapter 9	Additional File Handling	10 quizzes
Chapter 10	Numerical Applications	10 quizzes

MIDTERM AND FINAL EXAMS

Two midterm exams and two final exams are included, in a form
that can easily be copied for class distribution as either actual
exams or as practice exams. Solution for these exams are also
included.

A diskette containing all the quiz files and exam files is also
available upon request to the publisher.

QUIZ BANK

for

STRUCTURED FORTRAN 77 FOR ENGINEERS AND SCIENTISTS

Second Edition, by D. M. Etter

Quiz 1 - Chapter 1

Name:_____   Date:_____

CIRCLE THE CORRECT ANSWER

Answers from computers

a) are always correct because computer don't make mistakes

b) are correct if there are no syntax errors in the program

c) need to be checked by hand (or with a calculator) for a
    variety of data sets to be certain the program is
    running correctly

d) can be considered correct if the first answer from the
    computer was double checked by hand

Quiz 2 - Chapter 1

Name:_____   Date:_____

CIRCLE THE CORRECT ANSWER

A compiler

a)   is a piece of hardware for interchanging different computer programs

b)   is a software program which converts a program written in a high level language into machine code instructions

c)   is a low level language for controlling a piece of hardware

d)   checks the program statements for logic errors

Quiz 3 - Chapter 1

Name:_____   Date:_____

CIRCLE THE CORRECT ANSWER

A syntax error

a) occurs during the execution of a computer program

b) is caused whenever we divide by zero in the program

c) will <u>not</u> keep the computer from beginning execution of
the program

d) is caused by misspellings in the program statements

Quiz 4 - Chapter 1

Name:_____   Date:_____

CIRCLE THE CORRECT ANSWER

An editor

a)   is a piece of hardware for interchanging different computer programs

b)   is a special program in the computer used to edit information in the computer

c)   is a software program which converts a program written in a higher level language into machine code instructions

d)   checks the program statements for logic errors

Quiz 5 - Chapter 1

Name:_____   Date:_____

CIRCLE THE CORRECT ANSWER

A logic error

a)   occurs during the execution of a computer program

b)   will keep the computer from beginning execution of
     the program

c)   is caused by misspellings in the program statements

d)   is detected by the compiler

Quiz 6 - Chapter 1

Name:_____   Date:_____

CIRCLE THE CORRECT ANSWER

An algorithm

a)   is a software program which converts a program written in a higher level language into machine code instructions

b)   is a sequence of steps used in solving a particular problem

c)   is a low level language for controlling a piece of hardware

d)   is a procedure the compiler uses in checking the program statement for syntax errors

Quiz 7 - Chapter 1

Name:_____   Date:_____

CIRCLE THE CORRECT ANSWER

Decomposition

a)   is caused whenever we divide by zero in the program

b)   refers to breaking a problem into a series of
     smaller problems

c)   is changing the source code into machine code by the
     compiler

d)   refers to the logic mistakes that cause a program
     to give wrong results

Name:_____   Date:_____

CIRCLE THE CORRECT ANSWER

A high level language program

a) is difficult to understand because it is written as 0s and 1s by the programmer

b) does <u>not</u> have to be processed by a compiler before the computer can execute the instructions

c) needs to be checked by hand (or with a calculator) for a variety of data types to be certain the program is running correctly

d) can be considered correct if the first answer from the computer was double-checked by hand

Quiz 9 - Chapter 1

Name:_____   Date:_____

What words do the following acronyms represent?

FORTRAN

ALU

CPU

CRT

I/O

Quiz 10 - Chapter 1

Name:_____   Date:_____

CIRCLE THE CORRECT ANSWER

The three parts of the CPU are

a)   CRT, processing unit, internal memory

b)   ALU, processing unit, internal memory

c)   input, output, external memory

d)   ALU, processing unit, CRT

e)   compiler, program, editor

Name:_____   Date:_____

Convert the following formula to a FORTRAN assignment statement. The variable names ELTRNS, EG, ID, and IS represent single variables, not the product of two or more variables multiplied times each other. (T, B, and K are also variables.) Be careful to use the correct constant types in the expression and to use intrinsic functions where possible.

$$ELTRNS = \frac{T^{(ID/IS)} * B * e^{(-EG/2k)}}{LOG_{10}k * \sqrt{ID * IS}}$$

Name:_____   Date:_____

Convert the following formula to a FORTRAN assignment statement. The variable names DEN, VIS, and CF represent single variables, not the product of two or more variables multiplied times each other. (F and T are also variables.) Be careful to use the correct constant types in the expression.

$$DEN = \frac{CF(1.015 + 0.85F)^{0.832} * VIS^{CF}}{T(1.0 - CF)^{F}} + 5.03$$

Name:_____   Date:_____

Convert the following formula to a FORTRAN assignment
statement. Be careful to use the correct constant types in
the expression and to use intrinsic functions where
possible.

$$W = X * \arctan(X + \sqrt{A}) - \frac{A * \ln(X^2 + A^2)}{2}$$

Name:_____   Date:_____

Convert the following formula to a FORTRAN assignment statement. Be careful to use the correct constant types in the expression and to use intrinsic functions where possible.

$$ t = \frac{\sin^3 w * \cos^2 v}{5p + \ln v} + e^{-(v\ *w)/2p} $$

Name:_____   Date:_____

Convert the following formula to a FORTRAN assignment statement. Be careful to use the correct constant types in the expression and to use intrinsic functions where possible.

$$\text{FREQ} = \frac{(1 + \sin^3 A) * e^{-(A(2 + B))}}{B * \cos(A/2)}$$

Name:_____   Date:_____

Convert the following formula to a FORTRAN assignment statement. Be careful to use the correct constant types in the expression and to use intrinsic functions where possible.

$$J = \log_{10}H + 0.622P \left[\frac{1}{P - X} - \frac{1}{P + Y} \right]$$

Quiz 7 - Chapter 2

Name:_____   Date:_____

Convert the following formula to a FORTRAN assignment statement. Be careful to use the correct constant types in the expression and to use intrinsic functions where possible.

$$F = 0.35 \times 10^{-4} * \frac{X * (Y2 - Y1)^{2.5}}{2 \log_{10}(Y2 + \sqrt{Y1})}$$

Quiz 8 - Chapter 2

Name:_____   Date:_____

What is the result of the following FORTRAN statements?
(Write answer in <u>correct form</u> as either a Real or Integer
value, i.e. with or without the decimal point and decimal
portion. Show all your work for possible partial credit.)


```
REAL  X, A
INTEGER  I, J
I = 10
J = 4 + I
X = 9.0
A = 2*(J/I)+X**1.0/2.0
```


        Value of A is _____

Name:_____   Date:_____

What is the result of the following FORTRAN statements? (Write answer in <u>correct form</u> as either a Real or Integer value, i.e. with or without the decimal point and decimal portion. Show all your work for possible partial credit.)

```
REAL  A, B, C
INTEGER E
B = REAL(7/6)
C = 12.0
E = 6
A = 11.0*(C*B)/(C-B) + REAL(E)
```

Value of A is _____

Name:_____   Date:_____

What is the result of the following FORTRAN statements? (Write answer in correct form as either a Real or Integer value, i.e. with or without the decimal point and decimal portion. Show all your work for possible partial credit.)

```
REAL  X
INTEGER  I, J, N
I = 3
J = 2
X = 1.5
N = X - REAL(I)/X + REAL(J**I/J) + 10/3
```

Value of N is _____

Name:_____   Date:_____

Complete the following FORTRAN statements by writing a list directed output statement to print out the value of PI after it is calculated. Your output should include a <u>label</u> for the variable you are printing and the value of the variable.

```
    REAL  PI
    PI = 4.0*ATAN(1.0)
*
*   Print out the calculated value of PI
*
```

Quiz 12 - Chapter 2

Name:_____   Date:_____

Complete the following FORTRAN statements by writing a list directed output statement to print out the value of E after it is calculated. Your output should include a label for the variable you are printing and the value of the variable.

```
      REAL E
      E = EXP(1.0)
*
*  Print out the calculated value of e
*
```

Name:_____   Date:_____

    <u>CAREFULLY</u> show the results of the following PRINT statement. Use the character '␣' below the output line to show the horizontal spacing.

```
      REAL  R
      INTEGER  KNT
      R = 1545.34
      KNT = -124
      PRINT 10, R, KNT, R
   10 FORMAT (3X, F8.3, 3X, I3, 3X, E11.4)
```

Name:_____   Date:_____

CAREFULLY show the results of the following PRINT statement. Use the character 'ϸ' below the output line to show the horizontal spacing.

```
      REAL  X1, Y1
      INTEGER  CNT
      X1 = 0.001248
      Y1 = X1 + 2.0
      CNT = 2
      PRINT 10, X1, Y1, CNT
   10 FORMAT (3X, E12.5, 3X, F7.3, 3X, I5)
```

Name:_____   Date:_____

CAREFULLY show the results of the following PRINT statement. Use the character '∅' below the output line to show the horizontal spacing.


```
      REAL  X, R
      X = 198.45
      R = 6.023E+23
      PRINT 10, X, R, X
   10 FORMAT (3X, F7.5, 2X, E11.4, 3X, F7.3)
```

Name:_____   Date:_____

CIRCLE THE CORRECT ANSWER(S)

Which following IF statement groups contain <u>valid</u> syntax?
(Read the statements <u>very</u> carefully. Any small error would
cause the compiler to reject the statement(s).)

```
a)      IF (A.GT.0.0) B = X**2
        ENDIF

b)      IF (A.NOT.0.0) THEN
             C = D**E
             B = X**2
        END
c)      IF (A.GT.0.0) THEN
             A = 0.0
        ELSE THEN
             B = A**2
             C = D**E
        ENDIF

d)      IF (A.GT.10.0) THEN
             C = D**E
        ELSEIF (A.GT.0.0) THEN
             C = D**(E/2.0)
             B = X**1.5
        ENDIF
```

Quiz 2 - Chapter 3

Name:_____   Date:_____

CIRCLE THE CORRECT ANSWER(S)

Which following IF statements groups contain <u>valid</u> syntax?
(Read the statements <u>very</u> carefully. Any small error would
cause the compiler to reject the statement(s).)

```
        a)      IF (A.NOT.0.0) THEN
                    C = D**E
                    B = X**2

        b)      IF (A.GT.0.0) THEN
                    A = 0.0
                ELSE
                    B = A**2
                    C = D**E
                ENDIF

        c)      IF (A.GT.0.0) B = X**2

        d)      IF (A.GT.10.0) THEN
                    C = D**E
                ELSEIF (A.GT.0.0) ELSE
                    C = D**(E/2.0)
                    B = X**1.5
                ENDIF
```

Quiz 3 - Chapter 3

Name:_____   Date:_____

CIRCLE THE CORRECT ANSWER(S)

Which following IF statements groups contain <u>valid</u> syntax?
(Read the statements <u>very</u> carefully. Any small error would
cause the compiler to reject the statement(s).)

```
    a)      IF (A.GT.10.0) THEN
                C = D**E
            ELSE (A.GT.0.0)   THEN
                C = D**(E/2.0)
                B = X**1.5
            ENDIF

    b)      IF (A.GT.0.0) B = X**2

    c)      IF (A.NOT.0.0) THEN
                C = D**E
                B = X**2
            ENDIF

    d)      IF (A.GT.0.0) THEN
                A = 0.0
            ELSE THEN
                B = A**2
                C = D**E
            ENDIF
```

Name:_____   Date:_____

CIRCLE THE CORRECT ANSWER(S)

Which following IF statements groups contain <u>valid</u> syntax?
(Read the statements <u>very</u> carefully. Any small error would
cause the compiler to reject the statment(s).)

```
a)      IF (A.NOT.0.0) THEN
             A = 0.0
        ELSE
             B = A**2
             C = D**E
        ENDIF

b)      IF (A.GT.10.0) THEN
             C = D**E
        ELSEIF (A.GT.0.0) THEN
             C = D**(E/2.0)
             B = X**1.5
        ENDIF

c)      IF (A.GT.0.0) THEN B = X**2

d)      IF (A.GT.0.0) THEN
             IF (B.LT.50.0) THEN
                C = D**E
                B = X**2
             ENDIF
        ENDIF
```

Quiz 5 - Chapter 3

Name:_____   Date:_____

Write a FORTRAN IF type structure to perform the following.

1. If PRESS is more than 50.0 and the logical variable HOT
    is .TRUE., set the logical variables ALARM and DANGER
    to .TRUE.
2. If PRESS is less than or equal to 50.0 and HOT is
    .TRUE., set ALARM to .FALSE. and DANGER to .TRUE.
3. If PRESS is more than 50.0 but HOT is .FALSE., set ALARM
    to .FALSE. and DANGER to .TRUE.
4. Else if none of the above conditions are satisfied,
    set both ALARM and DANGER to .FALSE.

Name:_____   Date:_____

Write a FORTRAN IF type structure to perform the following.

1. If the logical variable BRITLE is .TRUE. and the ratio
    of LOAD to STRESS is greater than 1.0, set the logical
    variables ALARM and DANGER to .TRUE.
2. If BRITLE is .FALSE. and the ratio of LOAD to STRESS is
    greater than 1.0, set ALARM to .FALSE. and DANGER to
    .TRUE.
3. If BRITTLE is .TRUE. and the ratio of LOAD to STRESS is
    less than or equal to 1.0, set ALARM to .FALSE. and
    DANGER to .TRUE.
4. Else if none of the above conditions are satisfied,
    set both ALARM and DANGER to .FALSE.

Quiz 7 - Chapter 3

Name:_____   Date:_____

How many values are added into SUM by the following group of statements?   (Read the statements <u>CAREFULLY</u>)

```
      REAL  SUM, XDATA
      INTEGER  CNT
      SUM = 0.0
      CNT = 17
10 IF (CNT.GE.0) THEN
          READ *, XDATA
          SUM = SUM + XDATA
          CNT = CNT - 2
          GO TO 10
      ENDIF
```

Quiz 8 - Chapter 3

Name:_____   Date:_____

How many values are added into SUM by the following group of
statements?   (Read the statements <u>CAREFULLY</u>)

```
      REAL  SUM, XDATA
      INTEGER  CNT
      SUM = 0.0
      CNT = 0
10 IF (CNT.LE.16) THEN
          READ *, XDATA
          SUM = SUM + XDATA
          CNT = CNT + 2
          GO TO 10
      ENDIF
```

Name:_____   Date:_____

How many values are added into SUM by the following group of statements? (Read the statements <u>CAREFULLY</u>)

```
    REAL  SUM, XDATA
    INTEGER  CNT
    SUM = 0.0
    CNT = 0
10  IF (CNT.LE.17) THEN
        READ *, XDATA
        SUM = SUM + XDATA
        CNT = CNT + 4
        GO TO 10
    ENDIF
```

Name:_____   Date:_____

How many values are added into SUM by the following group of statements?   (Read the statements <u>CAREFULLY</u>)

```
      REAL   SUM, XDATA
      INTEGER   CNT
      SUM = 0.0
      CNT = 17
  10  IF (CNT.GE.0) THEN
            READ *, XDATA
            SUM = SUM + XDATA
            CNT = CNT - 3
            GO TO 10
      ENDIF
```

Name:_____   Date:_____

Assume the variable JK is an integer variable. How many times will the statements in the DO loop be executed?

DO 10 JK = 40, 0, -1

Name:_____   Date:_____

Assume the variable XY is a real variable. How many times will the statements in the DO loop be executed?

```
DO 10 XY = .5, 6.3, .5
```

Name:_____   Date:_____

Assume the variable COUNTR is an integer variable. What is
the value of COUNTR after the DO loop is executed?

```
    J = 5
    COUNTR = 0
    DO 10 I = J + 1, 15, 3
         COUNTR = COUNTR + 1
 10 CONTINUE
```

Name:_____   Date:_____

Assume the variable COUNTR is an integer variable. What is the value of COUNTR after the DO loop is executed?

```
      COUNTR = 0
      DO 10 I = 12, 0, -2
          COUNTR = COUNTR + I
   10 CONTINUE
```

Quiz 15 - Chapter 3

Name:_____   Date:_____

What is the value of the integer variable L1 after the
following statements are executed?

```
        L1 = 0
        DO 100 I = 4, 20, 5
            IF (I .EQ. 10) L1 = I**2
    100 CONTINUE
```

Name:_____   Date:_____

Assume the variables JK, LM, and COUNTR are integer
variables. What is the value of COUNTR after the following
nested DO loops are executed?


```
        COUNTR = 0
        DO 20 JK = 40, 0, -1
            DO 10 LM = 2, 10, 2
                COUNTR = COUNTR + 1
10          CONTINUE
20      CONTINUE
```

Name:_____   Date:_____

Assume the variables JK, LM, and COUNTR are integer variables. What is the value of COUNTR after the following nested DO loops are executed?

```
        COUNTR = 0
        DO 20 JK = -8, 12, 3
            DO 10 LM = JK + 8, 10, 2
                COUNTR = COUNTR + 1
10          CONTINUE
20      CONTINUE
```

Name:_____   Date:_____

Assume the variables JK, LM, and COUNTR are integer variables. What is the value of COUNTR after the following nested DO loops are executed?

```
        COUNTR = 0
        DO 20 JK = -8, -8, 3
            DO 10 LM = -22, 10, 2
                COUNTR = COUNTR + 1
10          CONTINUE
20      CONTINUE
```

Name:_____ Date:_____

Assume the variables JK, LM, and COUNTR are integer variables. What is the value of COUNTR after the following nested DO loops are executed?

```
        COUNTR = 0
        DO 20 JK = -80, 12, 30
            DO 10 LM = 2, 10, 5
                COUNTR = COUNTR + 1
10          CONTINUE
        COUNTR = COUNTR + 1
20      CONTINUE
```

Name:_____   Date:_____

The programmer who wrote the following code was surprised at the result it generated. What is the value of COUNTR after the following statements are executed?

```
      INTEGER JK, LM, COUNTR
          .
          .
      DO 20 JK = -80, 12, 30
         COUNTR = 0
         DO 10 LM = 10, 10, 5
            COUNTR = COUNTR + 1
10       CONTINUE
20    CONTINUE
```

Name:_____   Date:_____

Write a complete FORTRAN program for analyzing exam grades. The three exams grades for each student are contained in a file called RESLTS. Each line represents scores for EXAM 1, EXAM 2, and EXAM 3 for one student. Read the data into your program with a list directed READ statement. The last data line in the file contains the value -999 for all_three exams scores. Find the average score for each exam. Print them in the following format:

```
                AVERAGE SCORE

    EXAM 1          XX.XX
    EXAM 2          XX.XX
    EXAM 3          XX.XX
```

Name:_____   Date:_____

Write a complete FORTRAN program for analyzing exam grades. The three exams grades for each student are contained in a file called RESLTS. Each line represents scores for EXAM 1, EXAM 2, and EXAM 3 for one student. Read the data into your program with a list directed READ statement. The last data line in the file contains the value -999 for all three exams scores. Find the minimum score for each exam. Print them in the following format:

          MINIMUM SCORE

     EXAM 1   XXX
     EXAM 2   XXX
     EXAM 3   XXX

Quiz 3 - Chapter 4

Name:_____   Date:_____

Write a complete FORTRAN program for analyzing exam grades.
The three exams grades for each student are contained in a
file called RESLTS. Each line represents scores for EXAM 1,
EXAM 2, and EXAM 3 for one student. Read the data into your
program with a list directed READ statement. The last data
line in the file contains valid exam scores, so you will
need to use the END option to detect the end of the file.
Find the average score for each exam. Print them in the
following format:

          AVERAGE SCORE

     EXAM 1   XX.XX
     EXAM 2   XX.XX
     EXAM 3   XX.XX

Quiz 4 - Chapter 4

Name:_____   Date:_____

Write a complete FORTRAN program for analyzing exam grades.
The three exams grades for each student are contained in a
file called RESLTS. Each line represents scores for EXAM 1,
EXAM 2, and EXAM 3 for one student. Read the data into your
program with a list directed READ statement. The last data
line in the file contains valid exam scores, so you will
need to use the END option to detect the end of the file.
Find the minimum score for each exam. Print them in the
following format:

          MINIMUM SCORE

     EXAM 1   XXX
     EXAM 2   XXX
     EXAM 3   XXX

Name:_____   Date:_____

Write a complete FORTRAN program for analyzing exam grades. The three exams grades for each student are contained in a file called RESLTS. Each line represents scores for EXAM 1, EXAM 2, and EXAM 3 for one student. Read the data into your program with a list directed READ statement. The last data line in the file contains the value -999 for all three exams scores. Find the minimum score for each exam and the maximum score for each exam. Print them in the following format:

```
                MINIMUM SCORE          MAXIMUM SCORE

     EXAM 1         XXX                    XXX
     EXAM 2         XXX                    XXX
     EXAM 3         XXX                    XXX
```

Name:_____   Date:_____

Complete the following FORTRAN program to analyze data in the file HOURLY. There are 24 lines of data in the file. Each line contains two values, TIME and XDATA. Complete the following FORTRAN code to find the maximum XDATA value and its <u>associated</u> time. The data should be read in with an unformated read statement.

(*** Don't forget to complete the DO loop index limits ***)

```
      PROGRAM ANALYS
*
*     Program to find maximum XDATA value
*
      REAL  XDATA, XMAX
      INTEGER  TIME, TIMAX, I
      OPEN (UNIT = 3, FILE = 'HOURLY', STATUS = 'OLD')
*
*     Use the first set of values for the assumed
*     maximum value and associated time
*
      READ (3, *) TIMAX, XMAX
*
      DO 100 I = -1,
```

Name:_____   Date:_____

Complete the following FORTRAN program to analyze data in the file HOURLY. There are 24 lines of data in the file. Each line contains two values, TIME and XDATA. Complete the following FORTRAN code to find the minimum XDATA value and its <u>associated</u> time. The data should be read in with an unformated read statement.

(*** Don't forget to complete the DO loop index limits ***)

```
      PROGRAM ANALYS
*
*     Program to find minimum XDATA value
*
      REAL  XDATA, XMIN
      INTEGER  TIME, TIMIN, I
      OPEN (UNIT = 3, FILE = 'HOURLY', STATUS = 'OLD')
*
*     Use the first set of values for the assumed
*     minimum value and associated time
*
      READ (3, *) TIMIN, XMIN
*
      DO 100 I = 5,
```

Quiz 8 - Chapter 4

Name:_____   Date:_____

What values are assigned to the variables VOLTS, CURRNT, and
DAYS after the following READ statement is executed with the
data lines below?

```
        REAL   CURRNT, VOLTS
        INTEGER  DAYS
        READ 50, DAYS, VOLTS, CURRNT
    50 FORMAT (2X,I2,/11X,E11.4,/3X,F6.2)
```

Data Lines:

```
        4505914.094305.423E-04     {line 1}
        163204389174158.32E-23     {line 2}
        487-147957624875.19E-8     {line 3}
        ↑
        Col 1
```

Quiz 9 - Chapter 4

Name:_____   Date:_____

   What values are assigned to the variables AVG, SD, and NUM
after the following READ statement is executed with the data
lines below?


```
        REAL   AVG, SD
        INTEGER   NUM
        READ 50, AVG, NUM, SD
     50 FORMAT (F7.3, /19X, I3, /13X, E9.2)
```


   Data Lines:

```
        45.59148094305.423E-04      {line 1}
        163204389174158.32E-23      {line 2}
        487-147957624875.19E-8      {line 3}
        ↑
        Col 1
```

Quiz 10 - Chapter 4

Name:_____   Date:_____

What values are assigned to the variables X1, Y1, and NEW
after the following READ statement is executed with the data
lines below?


```
        REAL  X1, Y1
        INTEGER  NEW
        READ 50, X1, Y1, NEW
    50 FORMAT (3X, F6.2, 3X, E10.3, //3X, I3)
```

Data Lines:

```
        4505914.094305.423E-04      {line 1}
        163204389174158.32E-23      {line 2}
        487-147957624875.19E-8      {line 3}
        ↑
      Col 1
```

55

Name:_____   Date:_____

Draw the array and indicate the contents for each position in the array after executing the following set of statements. If no value is given for a specific position, fill it with a question mark.

```
    REAL  X(6)
    INTEGER  I
    DO 100 I = 6, 1, -1
        IF (I.GT.1) X(I) = REAL(9 - I) + 5.0
100 CONTINUE
```

Name:_____   Date:_____

Draw the array and indicate the contents for each position
in the array after executing the following set of
statements. If no value is given for a specific position,
fill it with a question mark.

```
        REAL  X(8)
        INTEGER  I
        DO 100 I = 1, 8
           IF (I.LE.3) THEN
              X(I+1) = REAL(I)**2
           ELSE
              X(I) = -2.5
           ENDIF
   100  CONTINUE
```

Name:_____   Date:_____

Draw the array and indicate the contents for each position
in the array after executing the following set of
statements. If no value is given for a specific position,
fill it with a question mark.

```
      REAL  Z(0:10)
      INTEGER  I
      DO 100 I = 10, 1, -1
         IF (I.GT.0) Z(I) = REAL(11 - I)
  100 CONTINUE
```

Quiz 4 - Chapter 5

Name:_____   Date:_____

Draw the array and indicate the contents for each position in the array after executing the following set of statements. If no value is given for a specific position, fill it with a question mark.

```
        REAL  X(8)
        INTEGER  I, J
        DO 100 I = 1, 14, 2
            J = (I + 1)/2
            IF (I.LE.7) X(J) = REAL(I - J)
    100 CONTINUE
```

Quiz 5 - Chapter 5

Name:_____   Date:_____

Write the FORTRAN statements to help analyze the data in the
array Z. Assume that Z, a one dimensional array of 50 real
values has already been filled with data. Give the
statements necessary to count the number of positive values,
zero values, and negative values in the array. Then give
the FORTRAN statements to print out the results in the
following form:

                XX POSITIVE VALUES
                XX ZERO VALUES
                XX NEGATIVE VALUES

Name:_____   Date:_____

Write the OPEN and READ FORTRAN statements to read values from the file FLOOD into the array RAIN by rows. Assume you do not know the format of the data. Therefore, use a list directed READ statement. Additionally you will also <u>have</u> to use implied DO loo<u>ps</u> in a single READ statement. Read the data into the entire first <u>row</u> before putting additional data into the second <u>row</u>. The array RAIN is defined below.

(Hint: since you are reading data by rows, which subscript changes fastest?)

```
      REAL  RAIN(10,4)
      INTEGER  I, J
```

Name:_____   Date:_____

Write the OPEN and READ FORTRAN statements to read values from the file AVLNCH into the array SNOW by rows. Assume you do not know the format of the data. Therefore use a list directed READ statement. Additionally you will also <u>have</u> to use implied DO loo<u>ps</u> in a single READ statement. Read the data into the entire first <u>row</u> before putting additional data into the second <u>row</u>. The array SNOW is defined below.

(Hint: since you are reading data by rows, which subscript changes fastest?)

```
REAL  SNOW(10,6)
INTEGER  I, J
```

Name:_____   Date:_____

Draw the array and indicate the contents for each position in the array after executing the following set of statements. If no value is given for a specific position, fill it with a question mark.

```
      REAL  X(4,4)
      INTEGER  I, J
      DO 100 I = 1, 4
         DO 50 J = 1,  4
            X(I,J) = REAL(MOD(I*J,4))
  50     CONTINUE
 100 CONTINUE
      DO 150 I = 1,4,2
         X(I,3) = REAL (I)
 150 CONTINUE
```

Name:_____   Date:_____

Draw the array and indicate the contents for each position in the array after executing the following set of statements. If no value is given for a specific position, fill it with a question mark.

```
      INTEGER  I, J, X(4,4)
      DATA  X /16*0/
      DO 100 I = 1, 4
         DO 50 J = 1, 4
            IF (I.EQ.J) THEN
               X(I,J) = 1
            ELSEIF (I.EQ.5-J) THEN
               X(I,J) = -1
            ENDIF
 50      CONTINUE
100 CONTINUE
```

Name:_____   Date:_____

Give the statements necessary to fill a two-dimensional array VAL with values computed for the function

Specify the array for real values with 10 rows and 11 columns. Each row corresponds to a value of x from 1.0 to 10.0 and each column corresponds to a value of y from -5.0 to 5.0. For example, the element value for VAL(3,8) is determined by setting x equal to 3.0 and y equal to 2.0 in the above equation.

Quiz 11 - Chapter 5

Name:_____   Date:_____

Draw the array and indicate the contents for each position in the array after executing the following set of statements. If no value is given for a specific position, fill it with a question mark.

```
    REAL  A(3,5)
    INTEGER  I, J
    DO 100 I = 1, 3
        DO 50 J = 1, 4
            A(I,J) = REAL((J-1)*5+I)
 50     CONTINUE
100 CONTINUE
```

Quiz 12 - Chapter 5

Name:_____   Date:_____

What are the values of J and A(J) after the following
statements are executed?

```
REAL  A(25), X, Y
INTEGER  J
X = 52.35
J = INT(X/10.0)
Y = REAL(5*J)
A(J) = X - Y
```

Name:_____   Date:_____

Show the contents of the real array A after the following statements are executed:

```
REAL   A(3,5)
INTEGER  M, L
DO 20 M=1,5
    DO 10 L=1,3
        A(L,M) = REAL((L - 1)*5 + M)
10      CONTINUE
20 CONTINUE
```

Name:_____   Date:_____

Give the statements necessary to print the contents of two
real arrays, A and B. A has 4 columns and 4 rows; B has 2
columns and 4 rows. Print all of the first row of A and the
first row of B on the first output line, the second row of A
and B on the second output line, and so on. Use an implied
DO loop and a formatted WRITE statement. Assume that all
the values will fit in an F5.2 data field. Design your own
spacing.

Name:_____   Date:_____

What value is stored in SUM after the following statements are executed?

```
    INTEGER  I, J, K(5,3), SUM
    DO 10 I=1,5
       DO 5 J=1,3
          K(I,J) = I + J
 5     CONTINUE
10 CONTINUE
    SUM = 0
    DO 15 I=1,5
       SUM = SUM + K(I,2)
15 CONTINUE.
```

Quiz 16 - Chapter 5

Name:_____   Date:_____

Assume that an integer array NUM with 50 elements has been filled with data. Determine the number of values in NUM that are multiples of 5. (Review the MOD function if you are not already familiar with it.)

Name:_____   Date:_____

Assume that arrays A and B both contain 20 real values.
Write the FORTRAN statements to fill an array C of 20 real
values such that the first element of C contains the larger
of the two values A(1) and B(1), the second element of C
contains the larger of the two values A(2) and B(2), and so
on.

Name:_____   Date:_____

Assume that a two-dimensional array ITEM with 3 rows and 5 columns has been filled with integer values. Give the statements necessary to print the following information:

```
SUM OF ITEMS IN ROW 1 = XXXXX
SUM OF ITEMS IN ROW 2 = XXXXX
SUM OF ITEMS IN ROW 3 = XXXXX
```

Name:_____   Date:_____

Assume that a two-dimensional array ITEM with 3 rows and 5 columns has been filled with integer values. Give the statements necessary to print the following information:

   SUM OF ITEMS IN COLUMN 1 = XXXXX
   SUM OF ITEMS IN COLUMN 2 = XXXXX
   SUM OF ITEMS IN COLUMN 3 = XXXXX
   SUM OF ITEMS IN COLUMN 4 = XXXXX
   SUM OF ITEMS IN COLUMN 5 = XXXXX

Name:_____   Date:_____

Assume that you have a real array X with 10 rows and 10 columns. Give the statements to find and print the value from the array with the maximum absolute value.

Name:_____   Date:_____

Write a statement function TOTINC to convert three arguments
representing yards, feet, and inches to a grand total of
inches. For example TOTINC(3, 1, 8) would return the value
128.

Quiz 2 - Chapter 6

Name:_____   Date:_____

Write a statement function TOTDYS to convert two arguments representing weeks and days to a grand total of days. For example TOTDYS(5, 9) would return the value 44.

Name:_____   Date:_____

Write an integer function to calculate the rounded result of integer division. The function, IRNDDV, receives two arguments, the numerator (NUM) and the denominator (DEN). Normally integer division truncates all results. Your function returns an integer result which is rounded to the nearest integer value after the dividing NUM by DEN. For example, the result of IRNDDV(8,3) is an integer 3. If the result is exactly midway between two integer values, round the value up to the next highest value.

Hint: you can use intrinsic functions within your function.

Name:_____   Date:_____

Write a logical function to return a value based on the value of the arguments it receives. The function, BIGENG, has three arguments, A, B, C. If A is greater than B * C, or B is greater than A * C, or C is greater than A * B return a true value. If none of these criterion are satisfied, return a false value.

Name:_____   Date:_____

Write a logical function to return a value based on the value of the arguments it receives. The function, SMALL, has three arguments, A, B, C. If A is less than B/C, or B is less than A/C, or C is less than A/B return a true value. If none of these criterion are satisfied, return a false value.

Name:_____   Date:_____

Write a logical function to return a value based on the
value of the arguments it receives. The function, DIFFER,
has three arguments, A, B, C. If A is less than B - C, or B
is less than A - C, return a true value. If neither of
these criterion are satisfied then return a false value.

Name:_____   Date:_____

Write a logical function ASCEND to return a true value if the array A is in ascending order. The function receives two arguments, A and N. A is the real, one dimensional array of N elements. If the array is not in ascending order it should return a false value. The function should not sort the array nor alter any elements in the array nor change the value of N.

Name:_____   Date:_____

Write a logical function DESCND to return a true value if the array A is in descending order. The function receives two arguments, A and N. A is the real, one dimensional array of N elements. If the array is not in descending order it should return a false value. The function should not sort the array nor alter any elements in the array nor change the value of N.

Name:_____   Date:_____

Write a logical function to return a true value if the
values of all elements in the array are between a minimum
and a maximum value. The array, A, is composed of 50 real
elements. The function, BOUNDD, receives three arguments
in the following order: A, RMIN, and RMAX. RMIN is the
lower bound and RMAX is the upper bound. If the values of
all elements are between these two bounds, the function
should return a true value. If any of the values are
outside the range of these bounds, the function should
return a false value.

Name:_____   Date:_____

Sometimes a maximum value can occur more than once in a group of data. For example, two students can tie for the top score on an exam. Write an integer function MAXS to count the number of times an identical maximum value is found in a one dimensional array of real values. The function receives two arguments in the following order: A and N. A is the array name and N is the number of elements in the array.

Name:_____   Date:_____

Sometimes a minimum value can occur more than once in a
group of data. For example, two students can tie for the
low score on an exam. Write an integer function MINS to
count the number of times an identical minimum value is
found in a one dimensional array of real values. The
function receives two arguments in the following order: A
and N. A is the array name and N is the number of elements
in the array.

Quiz 12 - Chapter 6

Name:_____   Date:_____

Write a real function RANGE to find the range of values in an array of real elements. The range is the maximum value minus the minimum value of all elements in the array. The function receives two arguments in the following order: A and N. A is the name of the real, one dimensional array and N is the number of elements in the array.

Name:_____   Date:_____

Write a real function CUBERT to evaluate the cube root of a
real number X. X is the only argument CUBERT receives.

Name:_____   Date:_____

Write a <u>logical</u> function XOR to compute a new type of logical operation called an exclusive or. The exclusive or operation is done with two logical variable arguments. In the function XOR call these A and B, respectively. The exclusive or is true if either A or B is true. However, if both A and B are true or both A and B are false then the exclusive or result is false.

Name:_____   Date:_____

Write a <u>real</u> function CLOSE to find the value closest (or
nearest) to the average value of all the elements in an
array. The function receives two arguments in the following
order: A and N. A is the name of the real, one dimensional
array and N is the number or elements in the array.

Quiz 16 - Chapter 6

Name:_____   Date:_____

Write an arithmetic statement function to calculate the area
of a trapezoid given the two heights (H1,H2) and the base
(B).

Name:_____   Date:_____

What is printed after the following statements are executed?

```
      INTEGER  M(10), CALC
      DATA  M/5*2,5*10/
      PRINT*, CALC(M)
      END
      INTEGER  FUNCTION CALC(M)
      INTEGER  M(10)
      CALC = 0
      DO 5 I=3,7
          CALC = CALC + M(I)
    5 CONTINUE
      RETURN
      END
```

Name:_____   Date:_____

What is printed after the following statements are executed?

```
      INTEGER  K(5,5), SUM
      DATA  K/25*5/
      PRINT 5, SUM(K)
   5  FORMAT (1X,'ANSWER = ',I6)
      END
      INTEGER FUNCTION  SUM(K)
      INTEGER  K(5,5), I
      SUM = 0.0
      DO 10 I=1,5
         SUM = SUM + K(I,I)
  10  CONTINUE
      RETURN
      END
```

Name:_____   Date:_____

Write a function DEGR to convert a value in radians to
degrees. If the value in degrees is not between 0 and 360
degrees, convert it to an equivalent number of degrees that
is between 0 and 360 degrees. For example, DEGR(3.0*PI)
should return the value 180.0. Similarly, DEGR(-1.0*PI)
should return the value 180.0.

Name:_____   Date:_____

Write a function RADN to convert a value in degrees to
radians. If the value in radians is not between 0 and
2.0*PI radians, convert it to an equivalent number of
radians that is between 0 and 2.0*PI radians. For example,
RADN(540.0) should return the value of PI. Similarly,
RADN(-180.0) should return the value of PI.

Name:_____   Date:_____

Write a FORTRAN subroutine for adjusting the values of <u>all</u> elements in a real, one dimensional array. Shift all the values equally so the minimum value in the array is equal to zero. For example, if the lowest value in the array is 10.0, subtract 10.0 from the value of every element. Similarly, if the minimum value is -22.5, subtract -22.5 from every value. The subroutine is called by the main program with the statement:

    CALL ADJUST(A, N)

where A is the real array to be adjusted and N is the number of elements in the array.

Name:_____   Date:_____

Write a FORTRAN subroutine for adjusting the values of <u>all</u> elements in a real, one dimensional array. Shift all the values equally so the maximum value in the array is equal to zero. For example if the largest value in the array is 29.35, subtract 29.35 from the value of every element. Similarly, if the largest value in the array is -18.0, subtract -18.0 from every value. The subroutine is called by the main program with the statement:

    CALL SHIFT(A, N)

where A is the real array to be adjusted and N is the number of elements in the array.

Name:_____   Date:_____

Write a FORTRAN subroutine for adjusting the values of <u>all</u>
elements in a real, one dimensional array. Shift all the
values equally so the average value of all elements is 0.0 .
Assume the function AVERG(A, N) is available for finding the
average value of the real, one dimensional array A with N
elements. After the average value is obtained, subtract it
from every element value to adjust the array. For example,
if the average value is -22.8, subtract -22.8 from the
value of every element. The subroutine is called by the
main program with the statement:

     CALL ZEROAV(A, N)

where A is the real, one dimensional array to be adjusted
and returned and N is the number of elements in the array.

Quiz 4 - Chapter 7

Name:_____   Date:_____

Write a FORTRAN subroutine for adjusting the values of <u>all</u> elements in a one dimensional array. The array contains <u>only positive</u> real values. Divide each value in the real array by the maximum value in the array. This causes all the values to be scaled between 0.0 and 1.0 . The subroutine is called by the main program with the statement:

                    CALL SCALE(A, N)

where A is the real, one dimensional array of positive values and N is the number of elements in A.

Name:_____   Date:_____

Write a subroutine which prints the values in a one-dimensional array with N elements in the following format:

```
VALUES IN ARRAY
1.   XXX
2.   XXX
3.   XXX
     (and so on till all values are printed)
```

Assume that the subroutine is called with the following statement, where K represents the integer array with N values:

```
CALL PRTVAL(K,N)
```

Name:_____   Date:_____

Write a FORTRAN subroutine for adjusting the values of <u>all</u> elements in a real, two dimensional array. Shift all the values equally so the maximum value in the array is equal to zero. The two dimensional array contains 4 rows and 6 columns. For example if the largest value in the array is 29.35, subtract 29.35 from the value of every element. Similarly, if the maximum value in the array is -18.0, then subtract -18.0 from every value. The subroutine is called by the main program with the statement:

CALL SHIFT(B)

where B is the real, two dimensional array to be adjusted.

Name:_____   Date:_____

Write a FORTRAN subroutine for adjusting the value of <u>all</u> elements in a real, two dimensional array. The array contains 3 rows and 8 columns. The subroutine will be called with two arguments, B, the array name and LIMIT, the test value. If the value of an array element is <u>lower</u> than LIMIT, set the value equal to LIMIT. If the value is greater than or equal to LIMIT, do not change the value of the element. Perform this operation on every element in the array. The subroutine is called in the main program with the statement:

        CALL BOTTOM (B, LIMIT)

where B is the name of the real, two dimensional array, and LIMIT is the real, test value.

Name:_____   Date:_____

   Write a FORTRAN subroutine for selecting the contents of a
one dimensional array.   Your subroutine, called BIGARR,
has three arguments, A, B, and C, respectively.   Each of the
these is a real, one dimensional array of 50 elements.   Your
subroutine receives values for A and B, and determines the
values for the array C. Use the following criteria in
selecting the contents of C.   If the sum of all the elements
in A is greater than or equal to the sum of all the elements
in B, then every element of C should contain the same value
as every element of A. If the sum of all the elements in B
is less than the sum of the elements in A, then C should
contain the values from array B.

Name:_____   Date:_____

Write a FORTRAN subroutine for adjusting the value of <u>all</u>
elements in a real, two dimensional array. The two
dimensional array contains 6 rows and 4 columns. Shift all
the values equally so the maximum value in the array is
equal to zero. For example if the largest value in the
array is 29.35, then subtract 29.35 from the value of every
element in the array. Similarly, if the maximum value in
the array is -18.0, then subtract -18.0 from every value.
The subroutine is called by the main program with the
statement:

    CALL SHIFT(B)

where B is the real, two dimensional array to be adjusted.

Name:_____   Date:_____

Write a FORTRAN subroutine for adjusting the values of <u>all</u>
the values in a real, two dimensional array. The two
dimensional array will contain 6 rows and 4 columns. Shift
all the values equally so the average value of all the
elements is zero. First determine the average value of the
array. Then subtract this average value from the value of
every element in the array. For example if the average
value is 10.0, then subtract 10.0 from the value of every
element in the array. Similarly, if the average value is
-22.18, then subtract -22.18 from every value. The
subroutine is called by the main program with the statement:

      CALL ZERO (D)

where D is the real, two dimensional array to be ajusted.

Name:_____   Date:_____

Write a subroutine that converts each number in an integer
array with 10 rows and 10 columns to either 0 or 1. If the
value in an element of the array is even, replace it with 0;
if the value in an element of the array is odd, replace it
with 1. Thus, after calling the subroutine with the
following statement:

        CALL CHNG(B)

the array B would contain only zeros and ones. (Review the
MOD function if you are not already familiar with it.)

Name:_____   Date:_____

Write a FORTRAN subroutine for adjusting the values of <u>all</u>
elements in a real, two dimensional array. The array size
is 5 rows by 7 columns and contains <u>only positive</u> values.
Divide the value of each element in the array by the maximum
value in the array. This causes all the values to be scaled
between 0.0 and 1.0. The subroutine will be called in the
main program with the statement:

                    CALL SCALE(H)

where H is the real, two dimensional array to be adjusted.

Name:_____   Date:_____

Write a FORTRAN subroutine for adjusting the values of <u>all</u> elements in a real, two dimensional array. The array contains 3 rows and 8 columns. The subroutine is called with two arguments, B, the array name, and LIMIT, the test value. If the value of an array element is <u>greater</u> than LIMIT, set the value of the element equal to LIMIT. If the value is less than or equal to LIMIT, do not change the value of the element. Perform this operation on every element in the array. This subroutine is called in the main program with the statement:

CALL TOP (B, LIMIT)

where B is the real, two dimensional array, and LIMIT is the real, test value.

Quiz 14 - Chapter 7

Name:_____   Date:_____

Write a FORTRAN subroutine for adjusting the value of <u>all</u> elements in a real, two dimensional array. The two dimensional array contains 6 rows and 4 columns. Shift the value of every element equally so the lowest value in the array is equal to zero. For example, if the lowest value in the array is 10.0, then subtract 10.0 from the value of every element. 10.0. Similarly, if the minimum value is -22.5, then subtract -22.5 from every value. The subroutine is called by the main program with the statement:

CALL BIAS(A)

where A is the real, two dimensional array to be adjusted.

Name:_____   Date:_____

Write a subroutine that is called with the following statement:

    CALL MODIFY (X,N)

where X is a real array with N elements. The subroutine should reverse the order of the values in the array. For example, the first and last values in the array should be interchanged, the second and next-to-last values in the array should be interchanged, and so on.

Name:_____   Date:_____

Write a subroutine that receives an integer that represents a value in minutes. The subroutine should determine the corresponding number of days, hours, and minutes represented by the initial value. The subroutine is called with the following statement:

CALL TIME(TOTMIN,DAYS,HOURS,MIN)

For example, if TOTMIN = 80, then the subroutine should return a value of 0 for DAYS, 1 for HOURS, and 20 for MIN.

Name:_____   Date:_____

Write a subroutine that receives an integer that represents a value in inches. The subroutine should determine the corresponding number of yards, feet, and inches represented by the initial value. The subroutine is called with the following statement:

CALL LENGTH(TOTINC,YARDS,FEET,INCHES)

For example, if TOTINC = 80, then the subroutine should return a value of 2 for YARDS, 0 for FEET, and 8 for INCHES.

Name:_____   Date:_____

Write a subroutine that receives an integer that represents a value in days. The subroutine should determine the corresponding number of weeks and days represented by the initial value. The subroutine is called with the following statement:

CALL TIME(TOTDAY,WEEKS,DAYS)

For example, if TOTDAY = 80, then the subroutine should return a value of 11 for WEEKS and 3 for DAYS.

Name:_____   Date:_____

A one-dimensional array Y contains 100 real values that are greater than zero. These values represent experimental measurements that contain a small amount of interference, or "noise" that occurred during the experiment. One way to eliminate some of the noise is to replace small measurements with zero, thus assuming that these small measurements represented only noise. Write a subroutine that receives a real array Y of 100 positive values, and changes to zero any values less than 3% of the maximum value.

Quiz 20 - Chapter 7

Name:_____   Date:_____

Assume that a two-dimensional array with 10 rows and 10 columns of integers is received by a subroutine ROWMAX. The subroutine should determine and print the maximum value in each row of the array in the following format:

```
MAXIMUM OF ROW  1 IS XXXXX
MAXIMUM OF ROW  2 IS XXXXX
.
.
.
MAXIMUM OF ROW 10 IS XXXXX
```

The subroutine is called with the following statement:

```
CALL ROWMAX(N)
```

Write a simple FORTRAN function to find the location of the first blank in a character variable. The function receives a character string of length 25. The function only receives one argument and returns an integer value. Call the function START. For example, it might be used in a section of a program as follows:

```
        PROGRAM QUIZ
  *
        CHARACTER*25 TITLE
        INTEGER BLANK, START
  *
        TITLE = 'STRUCTURED FORTRAN 77'
        BLANK = START (TITLE)
```

(The value of BLANK is 11 after the function is invoked.)

Name:_____   Date:_____

Write a simple FORTRAN subroutine for replacing all the blanks in a character variable. Change the blanks in the character string to the asterisk character: '*'. The subroutine is called BLANK and receives only one argument, the character string. The length of the character variable is 25. Here's an example of using the subroutine in a main program.

```
        PROGRAM  QUIZ
    *
        CHARACTER*25  TITLE
        INTEGER  BLANK
    *
        TITLE = 'STRUCTURED FORTRAN 77'
        CALL STARS(TITLE)
```

(After the subroutine is called, the character string TITLE contains 'STRUCTURED*FORTRAN*77****'.)

Name:_____   Date:_____

Write a subroutine LTRS for filling a character variable
with the three initials of a person's name. The subroutine
receives four arguments in the following order: FIRST,
MIDDLE, LAST, and INITLS. Each of the arguments is a
character string. FIRST, MIDDLE, and LAST are character
string variables of length 25 which contain a person's
first, middle, and last names. The argument INITLS is a
character variable with a length of 3. This final argument
is determined by the subroutine. Do not alter the contents
of the first three argument in the subroutine. For example,
if the first three arguments were

    FIRST = 'JOSEPH', MIDDLE = 'CHARLES', LAST = 'LAWTON'

then the character string INITLS would contain 'JCL' after
the subroutine is invoked in the main program.

Quiz 4 - Chapter 8

Name:_____   Date:_____

Write a subroutine PLACE for placing a character variable
in another character string. The subroutine has three
arguments in the following order: TEXT, LETR, and POS. The
first two arguments are character strings of length 25 and
1, respectively. The third argument, POS, is an integer
value. This integer value indicates which position in TEXT
the variable LETR is to placed. This merely replaces
whatever character was already in that position. Here's an
example of using the subroutine in a main program.

```
            PROGRAM  QUIZ
     *
            CHARACTER  TEXT*25, LETR*1
            INTEGER  POS
     *
            TEXT = 'COMPUTER'
            LETR = 'M'
            POS = 4
     *
            CALL PLACE (TEXT, LETR, POS)
```

(After the subroutine is called, the character string TEXT
contains 'COMMUTER'.)

Name:_____   Date:_____

Write a function HUNDRD for counting the number of times the character string '100' appears within a character string. The function receives one argument, NUMBER, the character variable being checked for the occurrence of '100'.   The function is used in a main program in the following manner.


```
        PROGRAM   COUNT
*
        INTEGER   CNT, HUNDRD
        CHARACTER   NUMBER*9
*
        NUMBER = '910087100'
        CNT = HUNDRD(NUMBER)
```

(The value of CNT is 2 after the function is invoked.)

Name:_____   Date:_____

Write a subroutine, CLEANF, for removing any leading blanks
from a character variable passed to it.   For example, if
the character string '   NOW IS THE TIME' was passed to the
                       ^^^   ^   ^   ^
subroutine, the character string 'NOW IS THE TIME   ' would
be returned from it. If there are   ^   ^   ^   ^^^
no leading blanks, the subroutine should simply return to
the main program. Assume the character string passed to it
would never be longer than 100 characters.

Name:_____   Date:_____

Write a subroutine TRANSP for switching the letters 'HTE' anytime they occur <u>alone</u> in a character string. Change the letters to 'THE'. Be careful not to change this set of characters if it is imbedded anywhere inside another word. The subroutine receives one argument, TEXT, the character variable containing the characters to be checked. The subroutine should change the character string TEXT and return the altered string back in this variable.

Name:_____   Date:_____

Convert the following formula to a FORTRAN assignment statement for double precision calculations. Additionally, write the specification statement to make all the variables in the equation double precision variables. Finally, make sure you use double precision constants and double precision functions (or generic functions) throughout the FORTRAN code.

$$S = \frac{(X - Y)^2 * Y^X}{4.6 * \log_{10}\left[\dfrac{2X}{(X + Y)}\right]}$$

Name:_____ Date:_____

Convert the following formula to a FORTRAN assignment statement for double precision calculations. Additionally, write the specification statement to make all the variables in the equation double precision variables. Finally, make sure you use double precision constants and double precision functions (or generic functions) throughout the FORTRAN code.

$$Av = 0.1789C \left[(Dt/Do) - 1\right]^{0.758}$$

Name:_____   Date:_____

Convert the following formula to a FORTRAN assignment
statement for double precision calculations. Additionally,
write the specification statement to make all the variables
in the equation double precision variables. Finally, make
sure you use double precision constants and double precision
functions (or generic functions) throughout the FORTRAN code.

$$J = \log_{10}H + 0.622P \left[\frac{1}{P - X} - \frac{1}{P - Y} \right]^{2.5z}$$

Name:_____   Date:_____

Convert the following formula to a FORTRAN assignment statement for double precision calculations. Additionally, write the specification statement to make all the variables in the equation double precision variables. Finally, make sure you use double precision constants and double precision functions (or generic functions) throughout the FORTRAN code.

$$F = 0.35 \text{X} 10^{-4} \ast \frac{X \ast \sqrt{2G} \ast (Y2 - Y1)^{2.5}}{\log_{10}(Y2 + Y1)}$$

Name:_____   Date:_____

Convert the following formula to a FORTRAN assignment
statement for double precision calculations. Additionally,
write the specification statement to make all the variables
in the equation double precision variables. Finally, make
sure you use double precision constants and double precision
functions (or generic functions) throughout the FORTRAN code.

$$J = 1 + \frac{K*M*r\left[\dfrac{u}{r * D}\right]^{0.41}}{G}$$

Name:_____   Date:_____

Convert the following formula to a FORTRAN assignment statement for double precision calculations. Additionally, write the specification statement to make all the variables in the equation double precision variables. Finally, make sure you use double precision constants and double precision functions (or generic functions) throughout the FORTRAN code.

$$E = 1 + \frac{0.5(1 + r)\left[\dfrac{u}{v} - 1\right]^2}{(1 + r)[(u*v) - 1]}$$

Quiz 14 - Chapter 8

Name:_____   Date:_____

Assume that you have a complex array CX that contains 10 elements. Give the FORTRAN statements necessary to compute and print the real and imaginary parts of the values in the following format:

```
                  REAL      IMAGINARY
      1.        XXX.XX      XXX.XX
      2.        XXX.XX      XXX.XX
      .
      .
      .
     10.        XXX.XX      XXX.XX
```

Name:_____   Date:_____

Assume that you have a complex array CX of 100 elements. Write a function that will determine the maximum magnitude of the values in the array.

Quiz 1 - Chapter 9

Name:_____   Date:_____

Write a program to create a direct access file from a
sequential file. The direct access file, ODD, will contain
every other record from the sequential file, BASE, beginning
with the first record. Each record in BASE contains five
integer values and the file contains an unknown number of
records.

Quiz 2 - Chapter 9

Name:_____   Date:_____

Write a program to count the number of records in a file.
The program is to ask the user for the file name during
execution. Then the program will check to make sure the
file exists before it tries to read from it. If the file
does not exist, the program should print an appropriate
message and stop execution. However, if the file does
exist, the program should count the number of records in the
file by reading each record with a character string variable
of length 1. The record should be read with formatted
input.

Name:_____   Date:_____

Write a program to update the sequential file TASKS by removing records which are out of date. Each record contains a task number, a cost to date, and a completion date. The completion date is stored as two numbers. The first is the year and the second is the day of the year. December 31, 1989 would be 89 365 for example. The task is still under progress if the completion date is later than the current date. If the completion date is the same as or earlier than the current date, the task has been completed. Write the program to query the user for the current date from the terminal. The program should then copy the file out to a temporary file removing any completed tasks as it proceeds. Finally, copy all the records in the temporary file back into TASKS. Don't forget to delete the temporary file at the end of the program.

Name:_____   Date:_____

A refinery has just begun manufacturing a new chemical. It is important to keep careful records of the temperatures in a number of different instruments in the production process. These values are stored in a sequential data file TEMP. Each line in the data file contains an integer instrument number and the corresponding real temperature of the instrument. The last line in the data file contains an instrument number of 9999. Write a program to generate two new files from this one. One file LOW should contain all the information for instruments with temperatures less than 100.0 degrees. The other file HIGH should contain all the information for instruments with temperatures greater than or equal to 100.0 degrees. Both new files should contain the trailer record with the instrument number of 9999.

Name:_____   Date:_____

A refinery has just begun manufacturing a new chemical. It
is important to keep careful records of the temperatures in
a number of different instruments in the production process.
One file LOW contains information for instruments with
temperatures less than 100.0 degrees. Another file HIGH
contains information for instruments with temperatures
greater than or equal to 100.0 degrees. Each line in the
data files contains an integer instrumentation number and
the corresponding temperature. The last line in the data
files contains an instrument number of 9999. Write a
program to combine these two files into one file called
TEMP. The file TEMP should contain all the information from
LOW followed by all the information from HIGH. Be careful
that only one trailer record is included in the new file.

Name:_____   Date:_____

A refinery has just begun manufacturing a new chemical.   It
is important to keep careful records of the temperatures in
a number of different instruments in the production process.
These values are stored in a sequential data file TEMP.
Each line in the data file contains an integer instrument
number and the corresponding real temperature of the
instrument.   The last line in the data file contains an
instrument number of 9999.   Write a program to determine and
print the number of instruments with temperatures above the
average temperature of all the instruments together.   (Do
not use an array.   However, you may read the data file
twice.)

Name:_____   Date:_____

A refinery has just begun manufacturing a new chemical. It is important to keep careful records of the temperatures in a number of different instruments in the production process. These values are stored in a sequential data file TEMP. Each line in the data file contains an integer instrument number and the corresponding real temperature of the instrument. The last line in the data file contains an instrument number of 9999. Write a program to determine and print the percentage of instruments with temperatures below the average temperature of all the instruments together. (Do not use an array. However, you may read the data file twice.)

Name:_____   Date:_____

A refinery has just begun manufacturing a new chemical. It is important to keep careful records of the temperatures in a number of different instruments in the production process. These values are stored in a sequential data file TEMP. Each line in the data file contains an integer instrument number and the corresponding real temperature of the instrument. The last line in the data file contains an instrument number of 9999. Write a program to store this information in a direct access file, using the following format for the integer instrument number and the corresponding temperature:

FORMAT (I4,2X,F6.2)

Assume that the instrumentation numbers are between 1 and 500, and can be used as the direct access key. Note that the direct access file does not use the trailer record with an instrument number of 9999.

Name:_____   Date:_____

A refinery has just begun manufacturing a new chemical. It
is important to keep careful records of the temperatures in
a number of different instruments in the production process.
These values are stored in a direct access file TEMPDA.
Each record in the data file contains an integer instrument
number (also the direct access key that represents record
number) and the corresponding real temperature of the
instrument. These values were written to the direct access
file with the following format:

    FORMAT (I4,2X,F6.2)

Write a program to determine and print the number of
instruments with temperatures above the average temperature
of all the instruments together. The instrument numbers vary
between 1 and 500, but not all the numbers are necessarily
used in the data file. (Do not use an array. However, you
may read the data file twice.)

Name:_____   Date:_____

A refinery has just begun manufacturing a new chemical. It is important to keep careful records of the temperatures in a number of different instruments in the production process. These values are stored in a direct access file TEMPDA. Each record in the data file contains an integer instrument number (also the direct access key that represents record number) and the corresponding real temperature of the instrument. These values were written to the direct access file with the following format:

FORMAT (I4,2X,F6.2)

Write a program to determine and print the percentage of instruments with temperatures below the average temperature of all the instruments together. The instrument numbers vary between 1 and 500, but not all the numbers are necessarily used in the data file. (Do not use an array. However, you may read the data file twice.)

Name:_____   Date:_____

Various mathematical functions can be represented by infinite series. For example, the exponential function can be written as:

$$e^x = 1 + \frac{x^2}{2!} + \frac{x^3}{3!} + \ldots + \frac{x^n}{n!}$$

When series expansions involve factorials, it is often more efficient to use an iterative method to determine the result of each successive term. For the exponential series, the n + 1 term is related to the n term by the equation

    term(n+1) = term(n)*x/(n+1)

Thus the third term is determined by multiplying the second term by the value of x and then dividing by 3.0. Notice the first term in this series is 1.0.

Write a program for calculating the exponential value of a real value x. The program should ask the user for the value of x (from the terminal). Calculate the exponential value of x using 25 terms in the above series.

Name:_____   Date:_____

Various mathematical functions can be represented by infinite series. For example, the sin function can be written as:

$$\sin(x) = x - \frac{x^3}{3!} + \frac{x^5}{5!} - \frac{x^7}{7!} + \ldots\ldots$$

When series expansions involve factorials, it is often more efficient to use an iterative method to determine the result of each successive term. For the sin series, the n + 2 term is related to the n term by the equation

$$\text{term}(n+2) = \text{term}(n) * [-x2/(n+1)(n+2)]$$

Thus the fifth term is determined by multiplying the third term by the value of -(x*x) and then dividing by 20.0. Notice the first term in this series is x and the series only contains odd terms.

Write a program for calculating the sin of 2.5 using the first 25 (odd) terms in the above series.

Name:_____   Date:_____

Various mathematical functions can be represented by infinite series. For example, the cos function can be written as:

$$\cos(x) = 1 - \frac{x^2}{2!} + \frac{x^4}{4!} - \frac{x^6}{6!} + \ldots\ldots$$

When series expansions involve factorials, it is often more efficient to use an iterative method to determine the result of each successive term. For the cos series, the n + 2 term is related to the n term by the equation

$$\text{term}(n+2) = \text{term}(n)*[-x2/(n+1)(n+2)]$$

Thus the fifth term is determined by multiplying the third term by the value of -(x*x) and then dividing by 20.0. Notice the first term in this series is 1.0 and the series only contains even terms.

Write a program for calculating the cos of 2.5 using the first 25 (even) terms in the above series.

Name:_____   Date:_____

Write a program to read an angle in radians from the terminal. Compute the sine of the angle using both single precision and double precision. Print both values and the percent difference of the two values (relative to the single precision value).

Name:_____   Date:_____

Write a program to read a positive value X from the terminal. Compute exp(X) using both single precision and double precision. Print both values and the percent difference of the two values (relative to the single precision value).

Name:_____   Date:_____

Write a <u>logical</u> function DIAG for determining if a two dimensional array represents a diagonal matrix. The array is real and has 4 rows and 4 columns. The diagonal matrix is a particular type of square matrix. A square matrix is one which has the same number of rows as columns. A matrix is called a diagonal matrix if every element off the main diagonal has a zero value. The main diagonal in a square matrix runs from the upper left hand element to the lower right element. Every element in the diagonal has a row number equal to its column number. (The value of the elements on the main diagonal may be zero or nonzero.) The function's only argument is the array name. The function should return a true value if and only if the array represents a diagonal matrix. An example of a 4 X 4 diagonal matrix appears below.

$$\begin{bmatrix} 2.1 & 0 & 0 & 0 \\ 0 & -1.2 & 0 & 0 \\ 0 & 0 & 6.8 & 0 \\ 0 & 0 & 0 & 0.7 \end{bmatrix}$$

Name:_____   Date:_____

Write a function TRACE to calculate the trace of a square
matrix.   The square matrix is held in a two dimensional,
real array with 4 rows and 4 columns.   A square matrix is
one which has the same number of rows as columns.   The trace
of a square matrix is the sum of all elements on the main
diagonal.   The main diagonal in a square matix runs from the
upper left hand element to the lower right hand element.
The row position is equal to the column position for every
element on the diagonal.   The function's only argument is
the array name.   The trace of the following matrix is 3.7.

$$\begin{bmatrix} 2.6 & 0 & 0 & 0 \\ 0 & -1.2 & 0 & 0 \\ 0 & 0 & 1.6 & 0 \\ 0 & 0 & 0 & 0.7 \end{bmatrix}$$

Name:_____   Date:_____

Write a subroutine TRANS to create the transpose matrix of a
3 x 4 matrix. Both the orginal matrix and the transpose
matrix are represented by two dimensional, real arrays. The
number of columns in the transpose matrix is equal to the
number of rows in the orginal matrix. Additionally, the
value of the elements in the first row of the orginal matrix
become the element values in the first column of the
transposed matrix, and so on. A 3 x 4 matrix and its
transpose are shown below:

$$
\text{original matrix} \quad
\begin{bmatrix}
0 & 1 & 2 & 3 \\
4 & 5 & 6 & 7 \\
8 & 9 & 0 & 1
\end{bmatrix}
\qquad
\text{transposed matrix} \quad
\begin{bmatrix}
0 & 4 & 8 \\
1 & 5 & 9 \\
2 & 6 & 0 \\
3 & 7 & 1
\end{bmatrix}
$$

The subroutine TRANS has two arguments, A and T, both two
dimensional arrays. T is the transposed matrix of the A
matrix.

Name:_____   Date:_____

An upper-triangular matrix is defined to be a square matrix
in which all elements below the main diagonal are zero.
(The main diagonal is the diagonal consisting of elements at
locations (1,1), (2,2), and so on.)   Write a logical
function that receives an integer matrix of size N X N and
then determines if the matrix is upper-triangular or not.
If it is upper-triangular, the function should return a true
value; otherwise it should return a false value.

Name:_____   Date:_____

An lower-triangular matrix is defined to be a square matrix
in which all elements above the main diagonal are zero.
(The main diagonal is the diagonal consisting of elements at
locations (1,1), (2,2), and so on.)   Write a logical
function that receives an integer matrix of size N X N and
then determines if the matrix is lower-triangular or not.
If it is lower-triangular, the function should return a true
value; otherwise it should return a false value.

Solutions to Quizzes

Chapter 1
1. c
2. b
3. d
4. b
5. a
6. b
7. b
8. c
9. FORmula TRANslation
   Arithmetic Logic Unit
   Central Processing Unit
   Cathode Ray Tube
   Input/Output
10. b

Chapter 2
1.
```
        REAL  ELTRNS, T, ID, IS, B, EG, K, NUM, DEN
          .
          .
          .
        NUM = T**(ID/IS)*B*EXP(-EG/(2.0*K))
        DEN = ALOG10(K)*SQRT(ID * IS)
        ELTRN = NUM/DEN
```

2.
```
        REAL  DEN CF, F, VIS, T, NUM, DEN
          .
          .
          .
        NUM = CF*(1.015 + 0.85*F)**0.832*VIS**CF
        DEN = NUM/(T*(1.0 - CF)**F) + 5.03
```

3.
```
        REAL  X, A, W, TERM1, TERM2
          .
          .
          .
        TERM1 = X*ATAN(X + SQRT(A))
        TERM2 = A*LOG(X*X + A*A)/2.0
        W = TERM1 - TERM2
```

4.
```
        REAL  T, W, V, P, TERM1, TERM2
          .
          .
          .
        TERM1 = (SIN(W)**3*COS(V)**2)/((5.0*P) + LOGV)
        TERM2 = EXP(-(V*W)/(2.0*P))
        T = TERM1 + TERM2
```

```
5.          REAL  FREQ, A, B, NUM, DEN
            .
            .
            .
            NUM = (1.0 + SIN(A)**3)*EXP(-A*(2.0+B))
            DEN = B*COS(A/2.0)
            FREQ = NUM/DEN

6.          REAL  J, H, P, X, Y, Z, TERM
            .
            .
            .
            TERM = 1.0/(P - X) - 1.0/(P + Y)
            J = ALOG10(H) + 0.622*P*TERM

7.          REAL  F, X, G, Y2, Y1, NUM
            .
            .
            .
            NUM = X*(Y2 - Y1)**2.5
            F = 0.35E-04*NUM/(2*ALOG10(Y2 + SQRT(Y1)))

8.   6.5
9.   18.0
10.  6
11.         PRINT*, 'PI = ', PI
12.         PRINT*, 'E = ', E
13. bb1545.340bbb***bbbb0.1545e+04
14. bbb0.12480e-02bbbbb2.001bbbbbbb2
15. bb*******bbb0.6023e+24bbb198.450

Chapter 3
1.   d
2.   b, c
3.   b
4.   b, c, d
5.          IF (PRESS.GT.50.0.AND.HOT) THEN
                ALARM = .TRUE.
                DANGER = .TRUE.
            ELSEIF (PRESS.LE.50.0.AND.HOT) THEN
                ALARM = .TRUE.
                DANGER = .TRUE.
            ELSEIF (PRESS.GT.50.0.AND..NOT.HOT) THEN
                ALARM = .FALSE.
                DANGER = .TRUE.
            ELSE
                ALARM = .FALSE.
                DANGER = .FALSE.
            ENDIF
```

```
            IF (BRITTLE.AND.LOAD/STRESS.GT.1.0) THEN
                ALARM = .TRUE.
                DANGER = .TRUE.
            ELSEIF (.NOT.BRITTLE.AND.LOAD/STRESS.GT.1.0) THEN
                ALARM = .FALSE.
                DANGER = .TRUE.
            ELSEIF (BRITTLE.AND.LOAD/STRESS.LE.1.0) THEN
                ALARM = .FALSE.
                DANGER = .TRUE.
            ELSE
                ALARM = .FALSE.
                DANGER = .FALSE.
            ENDIF
```

7. 9
8. 9
9. 5
10. 6
11. 41
12. 12
13. 4
14. 42
15. 0
16. 205
17. 42
18. 17
19. 12
20. 1

Chapter 4
1.
```
      *-------------------------------------------------------------*
            PROGRAM  SCORES
      *
      *  This program computes the average scores from a set
      *  of three exams scores.
      *
            INTEGER  EXAM1, EXAM2, EXAM3, SUM1, SUM2, SUM, COUNT
      *
            OPEN (UNIT=9, FILE='RESLTS', STATUS='OLD')
      *
            COUNT = 0
            SUM1 = 0
            SUM2 = 0
            SUM3 = 0
      *
            READ (9,*) EXAM1, EXAM2, EXAM3
         10 IF (EXAM1.NE.-999.OR.EXAM2.NE.-999.OR.
          +    EXAM3.NE.-999) THEN
                COUNT = COUNT + 1
                SUM1 = SUM1 + EXAM1
                SUM2 = SUM2 + EXAM2
```

```
                  SUM3 = SUM3 + EXAM3
                  READ (9,*) EXAM1, EXAM2, EXAM3
                  GO TO 10
              ENDIF
      *
              PRINT 15
          15 FORMAT (1X, 10X, 'AVERAGE SCORE'//)
              PRINT 20, REAL(SUM1)/REAL(COUNT)
          20 FORMAT (1X, 'EXAM 1', 9X, F5.2)
              PRINT 25, REAL(SUM2)/REAL(COUNT)
          25 FORMAT (1X, 'EXAM 2', 9X, F5.2)
              PRINT 30, REAL(SUM3)/REAL(COUNT)
          30 FORMAT (1X, 'EXAM 3', 9X, F5.2)
      *
              END
      *-----------------------------------------------------------*

  2.  *-----------------------------------------------------------*
          PROGRAM  SCORES
      *
      * This program finds the minimum scores from a set
      * of three exams scores.
      *
          INTEGER  EXAM1, EXAM2, EXAM3, MIN1, MIN2, MIN3
      *
          OPEN (UNIT=9, FILE='RESLTS', STATUS='OLD')
      *
          READ (5,*) EXAM1, EXAM2, EXAM3
          MIN1 = EXAM1
          MIN2 = EXAM2
          MIN3 = EXAM3
      *
      10 IF (EXAM1.NE.-999.OR.EXAM2.NE.-999.OR.
         +    EXAM3.NE.-999) THEN
              IF (EXAM1.LT.MIN1)  MIN1 = EXAM1
              IF (EXAM2.LT.MIN2)  MIN2 = EXAM2
              IF (EXAM3.LT.MIN3)  MIN3 = EXAM3
              READ (9,*) EXAM1, EXAM2, EXAM3
              GO TO 10
          ENDIF
      *
          PRINT 15
      15 FORMAT (1X, 10X, 'MINIMUM SCORE'//)
          PRINT 20, MIN1
      20 FORMAT (1X, 'EXAM 1', 9X, I3)
          PRINT 25, MIN2
      25 FORMAT (1X, 'EXAM 2', 9X, I3)
          PRINT 30, MIN3
      30 FORMAT (1X, 'EXAM 3', 9X, I3)
      *
          END
      *-----------------------------------------------------------*
```

```
3.   *-------------------------------------------------------------*
           PROGRAM  SCORES
     *
     *  This program computes the avarage scores from a set
     *  of three exams scores.
     *
           INTEGER  EXAM1, EXAM2, EXAM3, COUNT, SUM1, SUM2, SUM3
     *
           OPEN (UNIT=9, FILE='RESLTS', STATUS='OLD')
     *
           COUNT = 0
           SUM1 = 0
           SUM2 = 0
           SUM3 = 0
     *
        10 READ (9, *, END=50) EXAM1, EXAM2, EXAM3
           COUNT = COUNT + 1
           SUM1 = SUM1 + EXAM1
           SUM2 = SUM2 + EXAM2
           SUM3 = SUM3 + EXAM3
           GO TO 10
     *
        50 PRINT 55
        55 FORMAT (1X, 10X, 'AVERAGE SCORE'//)
           PRINT 60, REAL(SUM1)/REAL(COUNT)
        60 FORMAT (1X, 'EXAM 1', 9X, F5.2)
           PRINT 65, REAL(SUM2)/REAL(COUNT)
        65 FORMAT (1X, 'EXAM 2', 9X, F5.2)
           PRINT 70, REAL(SUM3)/REAL(COUNT)
        70 FORMAT (1X, 'EXAM 3', 9X, F5.2)
     *
           END
     *-------------------------------------------------------------*

4.   *-------------------------------------------------------------*
           PROGRAM  SCORES
     *
     *  This program finds the minimum scores from a set
     *  of three exams scores.
     *
           INTEGER  EXAM1, EXAM2, EXAM3, MIN1, MIN2, MIN3
     *
           OPEN (UNIT=9, FILE='RESLTS', STATUS='OLD')
     *
           READ (9, *, END=50) MIN1, MIN2, MIN3
     *
        10 READ (9, *, END=50) EXAM1, EXAM2, EXAM3
           IF (EXAM1.LT.MIN1)  MIN1 = EXAM1
           IF (EXAM2.LT.MIN2)  MIN2 = EXAM2
           IF (EXAM3.LT.MIN3)  MIN3 = EXAM3
           GO TO 10
```

```
      50 PRINT 55
      55 FORMAT (1X, 10X, 'MINIMUM SCORE'//)
         PRINT 60, MIN1
      60 FORMAT (1X, 'EXAM 1', 9X, I3)
         PRINT 65, MIN2
      65 FORMAT (1X, 'EXAM 2', 9X, I3)
         PRINT 70, MIN3
      70 FORMAT (1X, 'EXAM 3', 9X, I3)
*
         END
*----------------------------------------------------------*
```

5.
```
    *----------------------------------------------------------*
         PROGRAM  SCORES
    *
    * This program finds the minimum scores from a set
    * of three exams scores.
    *
         INTEGER  EXAM1, EXAM2, EXAM3, MIN1, MIN2, MIN3,
        +        MAX1, MAX2, MAX3
    *
         OPEN (UNIT=9, FILE='RESLTS', STATUS='OLD')
    *
         READ (9,*) EXAM1, EXAM2, EXAM3
         MIN1 = EXAM1
         MIN2 = EXAM2
         MIN3 = EXAM3
         MAX1 = EXAM1
         MAX2 = EXAM2
         MAX3 = EXAM3
    *
      10 IF (EXAM1.NE.-999.OR.EXAM2.NE.-999.OR.
        +   EXAM3.NE.-999.0) THEN
            IF (EXAM1.LT.MIN1) MIN1 = EXAM1
            IF (EXAM1.GT.MAX1) MAX1 = EXAM1
            IF (EXAM2.LT.MIN2) MIN2 = EXAM2
            IF (EXAM2.GT.MAX2) MAX2 = EXAM2
            IF (EXAM3.LT.MIN3) MIN3 = EXAM3
            IF (EXAM3.GT.MAX3) MAX3 = EXAM3
            READ (9,*) EXAM1, EXAM2, EXAM3
            GO TO 10
         ENDIF
    *
         PRINT 15
      15 FORMAT (1X, 10X, 'MINIMUM SCORE', 10X, 'MAXIMUN SCORE'//)
         PRINT 20, MIN1, MAX1
      20 FORMAT (1X, 'EXAM 1', 9X, I3, 16X, I3)
         PRINT 25, MIN2, MAX2
      25 FORMAT (1X, 'EXAM 2', 9X, I3, 16X, I3)
         PRINT 30, MIN3, MAX3
      30 FORMAT (1X, 'EXAM 3', 9X, I3, 16X, I3)
    *
         END
```

```
6.            DO 100 I = -1, 21
                 READ (3, *) TIME, XDATA
                 IF (XDATA.GT.XMAX) THEN
                    XMAX = XDATA
                    TIMAX = TIME
                 ENDIF
         100 CONTINUE
     *
              END

7.            DO 100 I = 5, 27
                 READ (3, *) TIME, XDATA
                 IF (XDATA.LT.XMIN) THEN
                    XMIN = XDATA
                    TIMIN = TIME
                 ENDIF
         100 CONTINUE
     *
              END
```

8. DAYS = 5
   VOLTS = 4.1583e-20
   CURRNT = -147.95
9. AVG = 45.5914
   NUM = -23
   SD = 875.19E-8
10. X1 = 5914.0
    X2 = 5.423E-04
    NEW = -14

Chapter 5

1. ?   12.0   11.0   10.0   9.0   8.0
2. ?   1.0   4.0   -2.   -2.5   -2.5   -2.5   -2.5

3. ?   10.0   9.0   8.0   7.0   6.0   5.0   4.0   3.0   2.0   1.0

4. 0.0   1.0   2.0   3.0   ?   ?   ?   ?

```
5.            INTEGER  POS, NEG, ZERO, I
     *
              POS = 0
              NEG = 0
              ZERO = 0
     *
              DO 10 I = 1, 50
                 IF (Z(I).GT.0) THEN
                    POS = POS + 1
                 ELSEIF (Z(I).EQ.0) THEN
                    ZERO = ZERO + 1
                 ELSEIF (Z(I).LT.0) THEN
```

```
                  NEG = NEG + 1
             ENDIF


        10 CONTINUE
           .
           .
           .
           PRINT 20, POS
        20 FORMAT (1X, I2, ' POSITIVE VALUES')
           PRINT 30, ZERO
        30 FORMAT (1X, I2, ' ZERO VALUES')
           PRINT 40, NEG
        40 FORMAT (1X, I2, ' NEGATIVE VALUES')

6.         OPEN (UNIT=9, FILE='FLOOD', STATUS='OLD')
           .
           .
           .
           READ(9,*) ((RAIN(I,J), J=1, 4), I=1, 10)

7.         OPEN (UNIT=9, FILE='AVLNCH', STATUS='OLD')
           .
           .
           .
           READ (9,*) ((SNOW(I,J), J=1,6), I=1,10)

8.
    1.0    2.0    1.0    0.0
    2.0    0.0    2.0    0.0
    3.0    2.0    3.0    0.0
    0.0    0.0    0.0    0.0

9.
    1    0    0   -1
    0    1   -1    0
    0   -1    1    0
   -1    0    0    1

10.        INTEGER  I, J
           REAL   VAL(10,11)
           .
           .
           .
           DO 10 I=1,10
              DO 5 J=-5,5
                 X = REAL(I)
                 Y = REAL(J)
                 VAL(I,J+6) = EXP(X - Y)*SIN(3.0*X)*COS(0.5*Y)
        5     CONTINUE
       10 CONTINUE
```

11.

```
1.0    6.0    11.0    16.0    ?
2.0    7.0    12.0    17.0    ?
3.0    8.0    13.0    18.0    ?
```

12. J=5
    A(J) = 32.35

13.

```
 1.0     2.0     3.0     4.0      5.0
 6.0     7.0     8.0     9.0     10.0
11.0    12.0    13.0    14.0     15.0
```

14.
```
      REAL  A(4,4), B(4,2)
      .
      .
      .
      WRITE 5, ((A(I,J), J=1,4), (B(I,J),J=1,2), I=1,4)
    5 FORMAT (6(1X,F8.2))
```

15. 25

16.
```
      INTEGER  NUM(50), COUNT, I
      .
      .
      .
      COUNT = 0
      DO 10 I=1,50
         IF (MOD(NUM(I),5).EQ.0) COUNT = COUNT + 1
   10 CONTINUE
```

17.
```
      REAL  A(20), B(20), C(20)
      INTEGER  I
      .
      .
      .
      DO 10 I=1,20
         IF (A(I).GT.B(I)) THEN
            C(I) = A(I)
         ELSE
            C(I) = B(I)
         ENDIF
   10 CONTINUE
```

18.
```
      INTEGER  ITEM(3,5), I, J, SUM
      .
      .
      .
      DO 10 I=1,3
         SUM = 0
         DO 5 J=1,5
            SUM = SUM + ITEM(I,J)
    5    CONTINUE
```

159

```
                    PRINT 7, I, SUM
           7        FORMAT (1X,'SUM OF ITEMS IN ROW ',I1,' = ',I5)
          10 CONTINUE

19.        INTEGER  ITEM(3,5), I, J, SUM
             .
             .
             .
           DO 10 J=1,5
              SUM = 0
              DO 5 I=1,3
                 SUM = SUM + ITEM(I,J)
           5     CONTINUE
              PRINT 7, J, SUM
           7     FORMAT (1X,'SUM OF ITEMS IN COLUMN ',I1,' = ',I5)
          10 CONTINUE

20.        REAL  X(10,10), MAXVL
           INTEGER  I, J
             .
             .
             .
           MAXVL = X(1,1)
           DO 10 I=1,10
              DO 5 J=1,10
                 IF (ABS(X(I,J)).GT.ABS(MAXVL)) MAXVL = X(I,J)
           5     CONTINUE
          10 CONTINUE
           PRINT 15, MAXVL
          15 FORMAT (1X,'ARRAY ELEMENT WITH MAXIMUM ABSOLUTE',
            +          ' VALUE = ',F8.2)
```

Chapter 6

```
1.         INTEGER  INCHES, FEET, YARDS, TOTINC
           TOTINC(YARDS,FEET,INCHES) = (YARDS*3 + FEET)*12 + INCHES

2.         INTEGER  WEEKS, DAYS, TOTDYS
           TOTDYS(WEEKS,DAYS) = WEEKS*7 + DAYS

3.    *------------------------------------------------------------*
           INTEGER FUNCTION  IRNDDV(NUM,DEN)
      *
      *  This function rounds the calculation to the nearest integer.
      *
           INTEGER  NUM, DEN
      *
           IRNDDV = INT(REAL(NUM)/REAL(DEN) + 0.5)
      *
           RETURN
           END
      *------------------------------------------------------------*
```

```
4.    *-------------------------------------------------------------*
            LOGICAL FUNCTION   BIGENG (A,B,C)
      *
      *  This function returns a true value based on certain comparison
      *
            REAL   A, B, C
      *
            BIGENG = .FALSE.
            IF ((A.GT.B*C).OR.(B.GT.A*C).OR.(C.GT.A*B)) THEN
               BIGENG = .TRUE.
            ENDIF
      *
            RETURN
            END
      *-------------------------------------------------------------*

5.    *-------------------------------------------------------------*
            LOGICAL FUNCTION   SMALL(A,B,C)
      *
      *  This function returns a true value
      *  based on certain comparisons.
      *
            REAL   A, B, C
      *
            SMALL = .FALSE.
            IF ((A.LT.B/C).OR.(B.LT.A/C).OR.(C.LT.A/B)) THEN
               SMALL = .TRUE.
            ENDIF
      *
            RETURN
            END
      *-------------------------------------------------------------*

6.    *-------------------------------------------------------------*
            LOGICAL FUNCTION   DIFFER(A,B,C)
      *
      *  This function returns a true value
      *  based on certain comparisons.
      *
            REAL   A, B, C
      *
            DIFFER = .FALSE.
            IF ((A.LT.(B - C)).OR.(B.LT.(A - C))) THEN
               DIFFER = .TRUE.
            ENDIF
      *
            RETURN
            END
      *-------------------------------------------------------------*

7.    *-------------------------------------------------------------*
            LOGICAL FUNCTION   ASCEND (A, N)
```

```
*
*  This function returns a true value
*  if A is in ascending order.
*
      REAL  A(N)
      INTEGER  N, I
*
      ASCEND = .TRUE.
      DO 5 I = 1,(N - 1)
         IF (A(I).GT.A(I+1)) THEN
            ASCEND = .FALSE.
         ENDIF
    5 CONTINUE
*
      RETURN
      END
*------------------------------------------------------------*
```

8.
```
*------------------------------------------------------------*
      LOGICAL FUNCTION  DESCND (A, N)
*
*  This function returns a true value
*  if A is in descending order.
*
      REAL  A(N)
      INTEGER  N, I
*
      DESCND = .TRUE.
      DO 5 I = 1,(N - 1)
         IF (A(I).LT.A(I+1)) THEN
            DESCND = .FALSE.
         ENDIF
    5 CONTINUE
*
      RETURN
      END
*------------------------------------------------------------*
```

9.
```
*------------------------------------------------------------*
      LOGICAL FUNCTION  BOUNDD (A, RMIN, RMAX)
*
*  This function returns a true value
*  if A lies between RMIN & RMAX.
*
      REAL  A(50), RMIN, RMAX
      INTEGER  I
*
      BOUNDD = .TRUE.
      DO 5 I = 1,50
         IF ((A(I).LT.RMIN).OR.(A(I).GT.RMAX)) THEN
            BOUNDD = .FALSE.
         ENDIF
    5 CONTINUE
*
      RETURN
```

```
          END
     *-----------------------------------------------------------*

10.  *-----------------------------------------------------------*
          INTEGER FUNCTION  MAXS (A, N)
     *
     *  This function counts the number of times
     *  that a maximum value occurs.
     *
          REAL  A(N), MAXIM
          INTEGER  I
     *
          MAXIM = A(1)
          MAXS = 1
          DO 5 I = 2,N
             IF (A(I).GT.MAXIM) THEN
                MAXIM = A(I)
                MAXS = 1
             ELSEIF (A(I).EQ.MAXIM) THEN
                MAXS = MAXS + 1
             ENDIF
        5 CONTINUE
     *
          RETURN
          END
     *-----------------------------------------------------------*

11.  *-----------------------------------------------------------*
          INTEGER FUNCTION  MINS(A,N)
     *
     *  This function counts the number of times
     *  that a minimum value occurs.
     *
          REAL  A(N), MINIM
          INTEGER  I
     *
          MINIM = A(1)
          MINS = 1
          DO 5 I = 2,N
             IF (A(I).LT.MINIM) THEN
                MINIM = A(I)
                MINS = 1
             ELSEIF (A(I).EQ.MINIM) THEN
                MINS = MINS + 1
             ENDIF
        5 CONTINUE
     *
          RETURN
          END
     *-----------------------------------------------------------*
```

```
12.   *---------------------------------------------------------*
            REAL FUNCTION   RANGE(A,N)
      *
      *  This function finds the range of an array.
      *
            REAL  A(N), MAXIM, MINIM
            INTEGER  N, I
      *
            MAXIM = A(1)
            MINIM = A(1)
            DO 5 I = 2, N
               MAXIM = MAX (A(I), MAXIM)
               MINIM = MIN (A(I), MINIM)
          5 CONTINUE
      *
            RANGE = MAXIM - MINIM
      *
            RETURN
            END
      *---------------------------------------------------------*

13.   *---------------------------------------------------------*
            REAL FUNCTION   CUBERT(X)
      *
      *  This function calculates the cube root of the given x.
      *
            REAL  X
      *
            IF (ABS(X).EQ.X) THEN
               CUBERT = X**(1.0/3.0)
            ELSE
               CUBERT = -(ABS(X)**(1.0/3.0))
            ENDIF
      *
            RETURN
            END
      *---------------------------------------------------------*

14.   *---------------------------------------------------------*
            LOGICAL FUNCTION   XOR(A,B)
      *
      *  This function operates like an exclusive OR.
      *
            LOGICAL  A, B
      *
            XOR = A.OR.B
            IF (A.AND.B) XOR = .FALSE.
      *
            RETURN
            END
      *---------------------------------------------------------*
```

15.
```
*-----------------------------------------------------------------*
      REAL FUNCTION  CLOSE (A, N)
*
*  This funtion finds a value closest to the average.
*
      REAL  A(N), SUM, AVG, DIFF
      INTEGER  N, I
*
      SUM = A(1)
      DO 5 I = 2,N
         SUM = SUM + A(I)
    5 CONTINUE
*
      AVG = SUM/REAL (N)
      DIFF = ABS (AVG - A(1))
      DO 10 I = 2,N
         IF (DIFF.GT.(ABS (AVG - A(I)))) THEN
            DIFF = ABS(AVG - A(I))
            CLOSE = A(I)
         ENDIF
   10 CONTINUE
*
      RETURN
      END
*-----------------------------------------------------------------*
```

16.
```
      REAL  TRAP, H1, H2, B
      TRAP (H1, H2, B) = ((H1 + H2)/2.0)*B
```

17. 26

18. ANSWER =   25
            ^^^^

19.
```
*-----------------------------------------------------------------*
      REAL FUNCTION  DEGR(RAD)
*
*  This function converts radians to degrees.
*
      REAL  RAD
*
      DEGR = RAD*180.0/3.141593
      IF (DEGR.LT.0.0) DEGR = -1.0*DEGR
    5 IF (DEGR.GT.360.0) THEN
         DEGR = DEGR - 360.0
         GO TO 5
      ENDIF
*
      RETURN
      END
*-----------------------------------------------------------------*
```

```
20.    *-----------------------------------------------------------*
            REAL FUNCTION   RADN(DEG)
       *
       *  This function converts degrees to radians.
       *
            REAL   DEG
       *
            RAD = DEG*3.141593/180.0
            IF (RADN.LT.0.0) RADN = -1.0*RADN
          5 IF (RADN.GT.2.0*3.141593) THEN
              RADN = RADN - 2.0*3.141593
              GO TO 5
            ENDIF
       *
            RETURN
            END
       *-----------------------------------------------------------*

Chapter 7
1.     *-----------------------------------------------------------*
            SUBROUTINE   ADJUST(A,N)
       *
       *  This subroutine adjusts values in an array.
       *
            REAL  A(N), LEAST
            INTEGER  I, N
       *
            LEAST = A(1)
            DO 5 I = 2,N
              LEAST = MIN (A(I), LEAST)
          5 CONTINUE
       *
            DO 10 I = 1,N
              A(I) = A(I) - LEAST
         10 CONTINUE
       *
            RETURN
            END
       *-----------------------------------------------------------*

2.     *-----------------------------------------------------------*
            SUBROUTINE   SHIFT (A, N)
       *
       *  This subroutine adjusts value in an array.
       *
            REAL  A(N), MOST
            INTEGER  I, N
       *
            MOST = A(1)
            DO 5 I = 2,N
              MOST = MAX (A(I), MOST)
          5 CONTINUE
```

```
      *
          DO 10 I = 1,N
              A(I) = A(I) - MOST
       10 CONTINUE
      *
          RETURN
          END
```

--

3.

--
```
          SUBROUTINE   ZEROAV(A,N)
      *
      *  This subroutine adjusts the values in an array.
      *
          REAL  A(N), AVG
          INTEGER  I, N
      *
          AVG = AVERG(A,N)
          DO 10 I = 1,N
              A(I) = A(I) - AVG
       10 CONTINUE
      *
          RETURN
          END
```

--

4.

--
```
          SUBROUTINE   SCALE(A,N)
      *
      *  This subroutine adjusts values in an array.
      *
          REAL  A(N), MAXIM
          INTEGER  I, N
      *
          MAXIM = A(1)
          DO 5 I = 2,N
             MAXIM = MAX (A(I), MAXIM)
        5 CONTINUE
      *
          DO 10 I = 1,N
              A(I) = A(I)/MAXIM
       10 CONTINUE
      *
          RETURN
          END
```

--

5.

--
```
      SUBROUTINE   PRIVAL (K, N)
      *
      *  This subroutine prints an array K with N elements.
      *
          INTEGER  K(N), N, I
      *
```

```
            PRINT*,'  VALUES IN ARRAY'
            DO 5 I = 1,N
                PRINT 10, I, K(N)
         5 CONTINUE
        10 FORMAT(1X,I2,'.   ',I3)
      *

            RETURN
            END
      *------------------------------------------------------*
```

6.
```
      *------------------------------------------------------*
            SUBROUTINE  SHIFT (B)
      *
      * This subroutine adjusts the values
      * in a two dimensional array.
      *
            REAL  B(4,6), MAXIM
            INTEGER  I, J
      *
            MAXIM = B(1,1)
            DO 10 I = 1,4
                DO 5 J = 1,6
                    MAXIM = MAX (B(I,J), MAXIM)
         5      CONTINUE
        10 CONTINUE
      *
            DO 20 I = 1,4
                DO 15 J = 1,6
                    B(I,J) = B(I,J) - MAXIM
        15      CONTINUE
        20 CONTINUE
      *
            RETURN
            END
      *------------------------------------------------------*
```

7.
```
      *------------------------------------------------------*
            SUBROUTINE  BOTTOM(B,LIMIT)
      *
      * This subroutine adjusts the values
      * in a two dimensional array.
      *
            REAL  B(3,8), LIMIT
            INTEGER  I, J
      *
            DO 10 I = 1,3
                DO 5 J = 1,8
                    IF (B(I,J).LT.LIMIT) B(I,J) = LIMIT
         5      CONTINUE
        10 CONTINUE
      *
            RETURN
            END
```

```
     *-----------------------------------------------------------*
8.   *-----------------------------------------------------------*
          SUBROUTINE  BIGGAR(A,B,C)
     *
     * This subroutine determines the larger array to put in array C.
     *
          REAL  A(50), B(50), C(50), ASUM, BSUM
          INTEGER  I
     *
          ASUM = 0.0
          BSUM = 0.0
     *
          DO 5 I = 1,50
             ASUM = ASUM + A(I)
             BSUM = BSUM + B(I)
        5 CONTINUE
     *
          IF (ASUM.GE.BSUM) THEN
             DO 10 I = 1,50
                C(I) = A(I)
       10    CONTINUE
          ELSE
             DO 15 I = 1,50
                C(I) = B(I)
       15    CONTINUE
          ENDIF
     *
          RETURN
          END
     *-----------------------------------------------------------*

9.   *-----------------------------------------------------------*
          SUBROUTINE  SHIFT (B)
     *
     * This subroutine adjust values in a two dimensional array.
     *
          REAL  B(6,4), MAXIM
          INTEGER  I, J
     *
          MAXIM = B(1,1)
          DO 10 I = 1,6
             DO 5 J = 1,4
                MAXIM = MAX (B(I,J), MAXIM)
        5    CONTINUE
       10 CONTINUE
     *
          DO 20 I = 1,6
             DO 15 J = 1,4
                B(I,J) = B(I,J) - MAXIM
       15    CONTINUE
       20 CONTINUE
```

```
      *
      RETURN
      END

      *------------------------------------------------------------*
10.   *------------------------------------------------------------*
      SUBROUTINE   ZERO(D)
      *
      * This subroutine adjusts values in a two dimensional array.
      *
      REAL   D(6,4), SUM, AVG
      INTEGER   I, J
      *
      SUM = 0.0
      DO 10 I = 1,6
         DO 5 J = 1,4
            SUM = SUM + D(I,J)
   5     CONTINUE
  10 CONTINUE
      *
      AVG = SUM/24.0
      DO 20 I = 1,6
         DO 15 J = 1,4
            D(I,J) = D(I,J) - AVG
  15     CONTINUE
  20 CONTINUE
      *
      RETURN
      END
      *------------------------------------------------------------*
11.   *------------------------------------------------------------*
      SUBROUTINE   CHNG(B)
      *
      * This subroutine converts values to zeros and ones.
      *
      INTEGER   B(10,10), I, J
      *
      DO 10 I=1,10
         DO 5 J=1,10
            IF (MOD(B(I,J),2).EQ.0) THEN
               B(I,J) = 0
            ELSE
               B(I,J) = 1
            ENDIF
   5     CONTINUE
  10 CONTINUE
      *
      RETURN
      END
      *------------------------------------------------------------*
```

```
12. *-----------------------------------------------------------*
          SUBROUTINE   SCALE(H)
      *
      * This subroutine adjusts values in a two dimensional array.
      *
          REAL  H(5,7), MAXIM
          INTEGER  I, J
      *
          MAXIM = H(1,1)
          DO 10 I = 1,5
             DO 5 J = 1,7
                MAXIM = MAX (H(I,J), MAXIM)
       5     CONTINUE
      10 CONTINUE
      *
          DO 20 I = 1,5
             DO 15 J = 1,7
                H(I,J) = H(I,J)/MAXIM
      15     CONTINUE
      20 CONTINUE
      *
          RETURN
          END
      *-----------------------------------------------------------*

13. *-----------------------------------------------------------*
          SUBROUTINE   TOP (B, LIMIT)
      *
      * This subroutine adjusts values in a two dimensional array.
      *
          REAL  B(3,8), LIMIT
          INTEGER  I, J
      *
          DO 10 I = 1,3
             DO 5 J = 1,8
                IF (B(I,J).GT.LIMIT) B(I,J) = LIMIT
       5     CONTINUE
      10 CONTINUE
      *
          RETURN
          END
      *-----------------------------------------------------------*

14. *-----------------------------------------------------------*
          SUBROUTINE   BIAS(A)
      *
      * This subroutine adjusts values in a two dimensional array.
      *
          REAL  A(6,4), MINIM
          INTEGER  I, J
      *
          MINIM = A(1,1)
          DO 10 I = 1,6
```

```
                DO 5 J = 1,4
                    MINIM = MIN (A(I,J), MINIM)
          5     CONTINUE
         10 CONTINUE
      *
             DO 20 I = 1,6
                 DO 15 J = 1,4
                     A(I,J) = A(I,J) - MINIM
         15     CONTINUE
         20 CONTINUE
      *
             RETURN
             END
      *------------------------------------------------------------*

15.   *------------------------------------------------------------*
             SUBROUTINE  MODIFY(X,N)
      *
      * This subroutine reverses the order of the values in an array.
      *
             REAL  X(N), TEMP
             INTEGER  I, N
      *
             DO 5 I = 1,INT (REAL(N)/2.0)
                 TEMP = X(I)
                 X(I) = X(N + 1 - I)
                 X(N + 1 - I) = TEMP
           5 CONTINUE
      *
             RETURN
             END
      *------------------------------------------------------------*

16.   *------------------------------------------------------------*
             SUBROUTINE  TIME(TOTMIN,DAYS,HOURS,MIN)
      *
      * This subroutine converts minutes to days,hours,minutes.
      *
             INTEGER  TOTMIN, DAYS, HOURS, MIN
      *
             DAYS = TOTMIN/1440
             HOURS = (TOTMIN - DAYS*1440)/60
             MIN = TOTMIN - DAYS*1440 - HOURS*60
      *
             RETURN
             END
      *------------------------------------------------------------*

17.   *------------------------------------------------------------*
             SUBROUTINE  LENGTH(TOTINC,YARDS,FEET,INCHES)
      *
      * This subroutine converts inches to yards,feet,inches.
      *
             INTEGER  TOTINC, YARDS, FEET, INCHES
```

```
       *
             YARDS = TOTINC/36
             FEET = (TOTINC - YARDS*36)/12
             INCHES = TOTINC - YARDS*36 - FEET*12
       *
             RETURN
             END
       *------------------------------------------------------------*
18.    *------------------------------------------------------------*
             SUBROUTINE   TIME(TOTDAY,WEEKS,DAYS)
       *
       *  This subroutine converts days to weeks and days.
       *
             INTEGER   TOTDAY, WEEKS, DAYS
       *
             WEEKS = TOTDAY/7
             DAYS = TOTDAY - WEEKS*7
       *
             RETURN
             END
       *------------------------------------------------------------*
19.    *------------------------------------------------------------*
             SUBROUTINE   SMOOTH (Y)
       *
       *  This subroutine smoothes noise in data.
       *
             REAL   Y(100), MAX
             INTEGER   I
       *
             MAX = Y(1)
             DO 10 I=2,100
                IF (Y(I).GT.MAX) MAX = Y(I)
        10 CONTINUE
       *
             DO 20 I=1,100
                IF (Y(I).LT.0.03*MAX) Y(I) = 0.0
        20 CONTINUE
       *
             RETURN
             END
       *------------------------------------------------------------*
20.    *------------------------------------------------------------*
             SUBROUTINE   ROWMAX(N)
       *
       *  This subroutine prints maximum of each row in N.
       *
             INTEGER   N(10,10), I, J, MAX
       *
             DO 10 I=1,10
                MAX = N(I,1)
```

```
            DO 5 J=2,10
               IF (N(I,J).GT.MAX) MAX = N(I,J)
       5    CONTINUE
            PRINT 8, I, MAX
       8    FORMAT (1X,'MAXIMUM OF ROW ',I2,' IS ',I5)
      10 CONTINUE
*
      RETURN
      END
*-----------------------------------------------------------*


Chapter 8
1.   *-----------------------------------------------------------*
            INTEGER FUNCTION  START(TITLE)
*
*    This function determines the
*    first blank in a character string.
*
      CHARACTER*25  TITLE
      INTEGER  CNT
*
      CNT = 1
    5 IF ((TITLE(CNT:CNT).NE.' ').AND.(CNT.LE.25)) THEN
         CNT = CNT + 1
         GO TO 5
      ENDIF
*
      IF (CNT.EQ.26) THEN
         PRINT*
         PRINT*,' NO BLANKS IN CHARACTER STRING'
         START = 0
      ELSE
         START = CNT
      ENDIF
*
      RETURN
      END
*-----------------------------------------------------------*


2.   *-----------------------------------------------------------*
            SUBROUTINE  STARS(TITLE)
*
*    This subroutine replaces blanks
*    in a character string with '*'.
*
      CHARACTER*25  TITLE
      INTEGER  I
*
      DO 5 I = 1,25
         IF (TITLE(I:I).EQ.' ') TITLE(I:I) = '*'
    5 CONTINUE
*
      RETURN
```

```
        END


        *------------------------------------------------------------------*
3.      *------------------------------------------------------------------*
        SUBROUTINE   LTRS(FIRST,MIDDLE,LAST,INITLS)
*
*  This subroutine finds a person's three initials.
*
        CHARACTER*25  FIRST, MIDDLE, LAST
        CHARACTER*3   INITLS
*
        INITLS(1:1) = FIRST(1:1)
        INITLS(2:2) = MIDDLE(1:1)
        INITLS(3:3) = LAST(1:1)
*
        RETURN
        END
        *------------------------------------------------------------------*

4.      *------------------------------------------------------------------*
        SUBROUTINE   PLACE(TEXT,LETR,POS)
*
*  This subroutine places a character in a string.
*
        CHARACTER   TEXT*25, LETR*1
        INTEGER   POS
*
        TEXT(POS:POS) = LETR(1:1)
*
        RETURN
        END
        *------------------------------------------------------------------*

5.      *------------------------------------------------------------------*
        INTEGER FUNCTION   HUNDRD(NUMBER)
*
*  This function counts the number of times a string appears.
*
        CHARACTER*(*)   NUMBER
        INTEGER   LENGTH, I, COUNT
*
        COUNT = 0
        LENGTH = LEN (NUMBER)
        DO 5 I = 1,(LENGTH - 2)
           IF (NUMBER(I:I+2).EQ.'100') COUNT = COUNT + 1
      5 CONTINUE
*
        RETURN
        END
        *------------------------------------------------------------------*
```

```
6.     *------------------------------------------------------------*
             SUBROUTINE   CLEANF(TEXT)
       *
       *   This subroutine removes leading blanks.
       *
             CHARACTER*100   TEXT
             INTEGER   POS, I
       *
             POS = 1
          5  IF (TEXT(POS:POS).EQ.' ') THEN
                 POS = POS + 1
                 GO TO 5
             ENDIF
       *
             DO 10 I = 1,(101 - POS)
                 TEXT(I:I) = TEXT(POS-1+I:POS-1+I)
         10  CONTINUE
       *
             RETURN
             END
       *------------------------------------------------------------*

7.     *------------------------------------------------------------*
             SUBROUTINE   TRANSP(TEXT)
       *
       *   This subroutine finds 'HTE' and replaces it with 'THE'.
       *
             CHARACTER*(*) TEXT
             INTEGER   LENGTH, I
       *
             LENGTH = LEN(TEXT)
             IF (TEXT(1:4).EQ.'HTE') THEN
               TEXT(1:3) = 'THE'
             ENDIF
       *
             DO 5 I=1,(LENGTH-4)
                IF (TEXT(I:I+4).EQ.' HTE ') THEN
                  TEXT(I+1:I+3) = 'THE'
                ENDIF
          5  CONTINUE
       *
             IF (TEXT(LENGTH-3:LENGTH).EQ.' HTE') THEN
               TEXT(LENGTH-2:LENGTH) = 'THE'
             ENDIF
       *
             RETURN
             END
       *------------------------------------------------------------*

8.     DOUBLE PRECISION   S, X, Y
           .
           .
           .
```

```
      S = ((X - Y)**2*Y**X)/(4.6D+00*DLOG10((2.0D+00*X)/(X + Y)))
```

9.
```
      DOUBLE PRECISION  AV, C, DT, DO
         .
         .
      AV = .1789D+00*C*(DT/DO - 1.0D+00)**.758D+00
```

10.
```
      DOUBLE PRECISION  J, H, P, X, Y, Z, PART
         .
         .
      PART = 1.0D+00/(P - X) - 1.0D+00/(P - Y)
      J = DLOG10(H) + .622D+00*P*PART**(2.5D+00*Z)
```

11.
```
      DOUBLE PRECISION  F, X, G, Y2, Y1, PART
         .
         .
      PART = X*DSQRT(2.0D+00*G)*(Y2 - Y1)**2.5D+00
      F = .35D-04*PART/DLOG10(Y2 + Y1)
```

12.
```
      DOUBLE PRECISION  J, K, M, R, U, D, G
         .
         .
      J = 1.0D+00 + (K*M*R*(U/(R*D))**.41D+00)/G
```

13.
```
      DOUBLE PRECISION  E, R, U, V, PART
         .
         .
      PART = .5D+00*(1.0D+00 + R)*(U/V - 1.0D+00)**2
      E = 1.0D+00 + PART/((1.0D+00 + R)*(U*V - 1.0D+00))
```

14.
```
         INTEGER  I
         COMPLEX  CX(10)
            .
            .
            .
         PRINT*, '              REAL      IMAGINARY'
         DO 10 I=1,10
            PRINT 5, REAL(CX(I)), AIMAG(CX(I))
       5    FORMAT (1X,I2,'.',6X,F6.2,4X,F6.2)
      10 CONTINUE
```

15.
```
      *-------------------------------------------------------------*
            REAL FUNCTION  MAXMAG(CX)
      *
      *  This function finds the maximum magnitude
      *  in a complex array.
      *
            COMPLEX  CX(100)
            INTEGER  I
      *
            MAXMAG = ABS(CX(1))
            DO 10 I=2,100
               IF (ABS(CX(I)).GT.MAXMAG) MAXMAG = ABS(CX(I))
         10 CONTINUE
```

```
      *
         RETURN
         END
      *------------------------------------------------------------*


Chapter 9
1.    *------------------------------------------------------------*
         PROGRAM   DIRECT
      *
      * This program converts a sequential file to a direct access file
      *
         INTEGER  NUM(5), CNT
      *
         OPEN (UNIT=1,FILE='BASE',STATUS='OLD')
         OPEN (UNIT=2,FILE='ODD',ACCESS='DIRECT',RECL=50,
        +      FORM='FORMATTED',STATUS='NEW')
      *
         CNT = 1
       5 READ (1,*,END=10) (NUM(I),I = 1,5)
           WRITE (2,*,REC=CNT) (NUM(I),I = 1,5)
           READ (1,*,END=10) (NUM(I),I = 1,5)
           CNT = CNT + 1
           GO TO 5
      10 CONTINUE
      *
         CLOSE (UNIT=1)
         CLOSE (UNIT=2)
         END
      *------------------------------------------------------------*

2.    *------------------------------------------------------------*
         PROGRAM   COUNT
      *
      * This program counts the number of records in a file.
      *
         CHARACTER  INPUT*25, CHAR*1
         INTEGER   CNT, ERROR
      *
         PRINT*
         PRINT*,' INPUT NAME OF FILE '
         READ (*,5) INPUT
       5 FORMAT (A)
         OPEN (UNIT=1,FILE=INPUT,STATUS='OLD',IOSTAT=ERROR)
      *
         CNT = 0
         IF (ERROR.EQ.0) THEN
      10    READ (1,5,END=15) CHAR
              CNT = CNT + 1
              GO TO 10
      15    CONTINUE
           PRINT*
           PRINT*,' NUMBER OF RECORDS IS ',CNT
```

```
            ELSE
              PRINT*
              PRINT*,'  *** ERROR, FILE NOT FOUND ***'
            ENDIF
      *
            END
      *----------------------------------------------------------*

3.    *----------------------------------------------------------*
            PROGRAM  UPDATE
      *
      *  This program updates a sequential file.
      *
            REAL  COST
            INTEGER  NUM, YEAR, DAY, INYEAR, INDAY
      *
            OPEN (UNIT=1,FILE='TASKS',STATUS='OLD')
            OPEN (UNIT=2,FILE='TEMP',STATUS='NEW')
      *
            PRINT*
            PRINT*,' INPUT CURRENT YEAR'
            READ*, INYEAR
            PRINT*
            PRINT*,' INPUT CURRENT DAY (1-365)'
            READ*, INDAY
      *
         5 READ (1,*,END=10) NUM, COST, YEAR, DAY
            IF (YEAR.GT.INYEAR) THEN
              WRITE (2,*) NUM, COST, YEAR, DAY
            ENDIF
            IF ((YEAR.EQ.INYEAR).AND.(DAY.GT.INDAY)) THEN
              WRITE (2,*) NUM, COST, YEAR, DAY
            ENDIF
            GO TO 5
        10 CONTINUE
      *
            CLOSE (UNIT=1,STATUS='DELETE')
            CLOSE (UNIT=2)
            OPEN (UNIT=1,FILE='TASKS',STATUS='NEW')
            OPEN (UNIT=2,FILE='TEMP',STATUS='OLD')
      *
        15 READ (2,*,END=20) NUM, COST, YEAR, DAY
            WRITE (1,*) NUM, COST, YEAR, DAY
            GO TO 15
        20 CONTINUE
            CLOSE (UNIT=1)
            CLOSE (UNIT=2,STATUS='DELETE')
      *
            END
      *----------------------------------------------------------*
```

```
4.  *----------------------------------------------------------------*
        PROGRAM  SPLIT
    *
    *  This program separates a data file.
    *
        REAL  TEMP
        INTEGER NUMBER
    *
        OPEN (UNIT=9, FILE='TEMP', STATUS='OLD')
        OPEN (UNIT=10, FILE='LOW', STATUS='NEW')
        OPEN (UNIT=11, FILE='HIGH', STATUS='NEW')
    *
        READ (9,*) NUMBER, TEMP
      5 IF (NUMBER.NE.9999) THEN
           IF (TEMP.LT.100.0) THEN
              WRITE (10,*) NUMBER, TEMP
           ELSE
              WRITE (11,*) NUMBER, TEMP
           ENDIF
           READ (9,*) NUMBER, TEMP
           GO TO 5
        ENDIF
    *
        WRITE (10,*) NUMBER, TEMP
        WRITE (11,*) NUMBER, TEMP
    *
        END
    *----------------------------------------------------------------*

5.  *----------------------------------------------------------------*
        PROGRAM  MERGE
    *
    *  This program combines a data file.
    *
        REAL  TEMP
        INTEGER NUMBER
    *
        OPEN (UNIT=10, FILE='LOW', STATUS='OLD')
        OPEN (UNIT=11, FILE='HIGH', STATUS='OLD')
        OPEN (UNIT=12, FILE='TEMP', STATUS='NEW')
    *
        READ (10,*) NUMBER, TEMP
      5 IF (NUMBER.NE.9999) THEN
           WRITE (12,*) NUMBER, TEMP
           READ (10,*) NUMBER, TEMP
           GO TO 5
        ENDIF
    *
        READ (11,*) NUMBER, TEMP
     10 IF(NUMBER.NE.9999) THEN
           WRITE (12,*) NUMBER, TEMP
           READ (11,*) NUMBER, TEMP
```

```
              GO TO 10


          ENDIF
      *
          WRITE (12,*) NUMBER, TEMP
      *
          END
      *-------------------------------------------------------------*
6.    *-------------------------------------------------------------*
          PROGRAM  CHECK
      *
      *  This program counts the number of
      *  above-average temperatures.
      *
          REAL  TEMP, SUM, AVE
          INTEGER  NUMBER, COUNT
      *
          OPEN (UNIT=9, FILE='TEMP', STATUS='OLD')
          READ (9,*) NUMBER, TEMP
          SUM = 0.0
          COUNT = 0
        5 IF (NUMBER.NE.9999) THEN
             SUM = SUM + TEMP
             COUNT = COUNT + 1
             READ (9,*) NUMBER, TEMP
             GO TO 5
          ENDIF
          AVE = SUM/REAL(COUNT)
      *

          REWIND (UNIT=9)
          COUNT = 0
          READ (9,*) NUMBER, TEMP
       10 IF (NUMBER.NE.9999) THEN
             IF (TEMP.GT.AVE) COUNT = COUNT + 1
             READ (9,*) NUMBER, TEMP
             GO TO 10
          ENDIF
      *
          PRINT 15, COUNT
       15 FORMAT (1X,I5,' TEMPERATURES ABOVE AVERAGE')
      *
          END
      *-------------------------------------------------------------*
7.    *-------------------------------------------------------------*
          PROGRAM  CHECK
      *
      *  This program computes the percentage of
      *  below-average temperatures.
      *
          REAL  TEMP, SUM, AVE
          INTEGER  NUMBER, COUNT, TOTAL
```

```
*

          OPEN (UNIT=9, FILE='TEMP', STATUS='OLD')
          READ (9,*) NUMBER, TEMP
          SUM = 0.0
          COUNT = 0
       5 IF (NUMBER.NE.9999) THEN
              SUM = SUM + TEMP
              COUNT = COUNT + 1
              READ (9,*) NUMBER, TEMP
              GO TO 5
          ENDIF
          AVE = SUM/REAL(COUNT)
          TOTAL = COUNT
*

          REWIND (UNIT=9)
          COUNT = 0
          READ (9,*) NUMBER, TEMP
      10 IF (NUMBER.NE.9999) THEN
              IF (TEMP.LT.AVE) COUNT = COUNT + 1
              READ (9,*) NUMBER, TEMP
              GO TO 10
          ENDIF
*

          PRINT 15, REAL(COUNT)/REAL(TOTAL)*100.0
      15 FORMAT (1X,F6.2,' PERCENT OF TEMPERATURES BELOW AVERAGE')
*

          END
*-----------------------------------------------------------*

8.    *-----------------------------------------------------------*
          PROGRAM   CREATE
*
*   This program converts a sequential file to direct access.
*
          INTEGER   NUMBER
          REAL   TEMP
*
          OPEN (UNIT=9, FILE='TEMP', STATUS='OLD')
          OPEN (UNIT=10, FILE='TEMPDA', STATUS='NEW',
         +         FORM = 'FORMATTED', ACCESS='DIRECT', RECL=12)
          READ (9,*) NUMBER, TEMP
       5 IF(NUMBER.NE.9999) THEN
              WRITE (10,15,REC=NUMBER) NUMBER, TEMP
      15      FORMAT (I4,2X,F6.2)
              READ (9,*) NUMBER, TEMP
              GO TO 5
          ENDIF
*
          END
*-----------------------------------------------------------*
```

9.   *---*
           PROGRAM   CHECK
     *
     * This program counts the number
     * above-average temperatures.
     *
           REAL   TEMP, SUM, AVE
           INTEGER   NUMBER, COUNT, I
     *
           SUM = 0.0
           COUNT = 0
           OPEN (UNIT=9, FILE='TEMPDA', STATUS='OLD',
          +   FORM='FORMATTED',ACCESS='DIRECT',RECL=12)
           DO 20 I=1,500
              READ (9,5,REC=I,ERR=20) NUMBER, TEMP
         5   FORMAT (I4,2X,F6.2)
              SUM = SUM + TEMP
              COUNT = COUNT + 1
        20 CONTINUE
           AVE = SUM/REAL(COUNT)
     *
           COUNT = 0
           DO 40 I=1,500
              READ (9,5,REC=I,ERR=40) NUMBER, TEMP
              IF (TEMP.GT.AVE) COUNT = COUNT + 1
        40 CONTINUE
           PRINT 55, COUNT
        55 FORMAT (1X,I5,' TEMPERATURES ABOVE AVERAGE')
     *
           END
     ---

10. *---*
           PROGRAM   CHECK
     *
     * This program computes the percentage
     * of below-average temperatures.
     *
           REAL   TEMP, SUM, AVE
           INTEGER   NUMBER, COUNT, I
     *
           SUM = 0.0
           COUNT = 0
           OPEN (UNIT=9, FILE='TEMPDA', STATUS='OLD',
          +   FORM='FORMATTED',ACCESS='DIRECT',RECL=12)
           DO 20 I=1,500
              READ (9,5,REC=I,ERR=20) NUMBER, TEMP
         5   FORMAT (I4,2X,F6.2)
              SUM = SUM + TEMP
              COUNT = COUNT + 1
        20 CONTINUE
           AVE = SUM/REAL(COUNT)

```
           TOTAL = COUNT
      *
           COUNT = 0
           DO 40 I=1,500
               READ (9,5,REC=I,ERR=40) NUMBER, TEMP
               IF (TEMP.LT.AVE) COUNT = COUNT + 1
        40 CONTINUE
           PRINT 55, REAL(COUNT)/REAL(TOTAL)*100.0
        55 FORMAT (1X,F6.2,' PERCENT OF TEMPERATURES',
          +          ' BELOW AVERAGE')
      *
           END
      *------------------------------------------------------------*
```

Chapter 10.

1.
```
      *------------------------------------------------------------*
           PROGRAM  SERIES
      *
      * This program calculates the series approximation of exponential.
      *
           REAL  TERM, EXPON, X
           INTEGER  I
      *
           PRINT*
           PRINT*,' INPUT VALUE OF X'
           READ*, X
      *
           TERM = X**2/2.0
           EXPON = 1.0 + TERM1
      *
           DO 5 I = 3,25
               TERM = TERM*X/REAL(I)
               EXPON = EXPON + TERM1
         5 CONTINUE
      *
           PRINT*
           PRINT*,'EXPONENTIAL VALUE OF X IS ', EXPON
      *
           RETURN
           END
      *------------------------------------------------------------*
```

2.
```
      *------------------------------------------------------------*
           PROGRAM SERIES
      *
      * This program approximates sin(x) using and infinite series.
      *
           REAL  SINE, X, TERM
           INTEGER  I
      *
           X = 2.5
           TERM = X
           SINE = TERM
```

```
      *
            DO 5 I = 2,48,2
               TERM = -TERM*X*X/(REAL(I)*REAL(I+1))
               SINE = SINE + TERM
          5 CONTINUE
      *
            PRINT*
            PRINT*,' THE APPROXIMATION TO SIN(2.5) IS ',SINE
      *
            RETURN
            END
      *------------------------------------------------------------*
```

3.
```
      *------------------------------------------------------------*
            PROGRAM  SERIES
      *
      *  This program approximates cos(x) using a infinite series.
      *
            REAL  COSINE, X, TERM
            INTEGER  I
      *
            X = 2.5
            TERM = 1.0
            COSINE = TERM
      *
            DO 5 I = 1,47,2
               TERM = -TERM*X**2/(REAL(I)*REAL(I+1))
               COSINE = COSINE + TERM
          5 CONTINUE
      *
            PRINT*
            PRINT*,' THE APPROXIMATION TO COSINE(2.5) IS ',COSINE
      *
            RETURN
            END
      *------------------------------------------------------------*
```

4.
```
      *------------------------------------------------------------*
            PROGRAM  CMPAR
      *
      *  This program compares single precision sine values
      *  to double precision sine values.
      *
            REAL  SP, ANGLE
            DOUBLE PRECISION  DP, DANGLE, PDIFF
      *
            PRINT*, 'ENTER ANGLE IN RADIANS'
            READ*, ANGLE
            DANGLE = DBLE(ANGLE)
            SP = SIN(ANGLE)
            DP = SIN(DANGLE)
            PDIFF = ABS(DP - DBLE(SP))/DBLE(SP)*100.00
```

```
          PRINT 5, PDIFF
        5 FORMAT (1X,'PERCENT DIFFERENCE = ',F8.4)
*
          END
*-----------------------------------------------------------*
```

5.
```
*-----------------------------------------------------------*
          PROGRAM  CMPAR
*
*  This program compares single precision exponential
*  values to double precision exponential values.
*
          REAL  SP, X
          DOUBLE PRECISION  DP, DX, PDIFF
*
          PRINT*, 'ENTER POSITIVE VALUE X'
          READ*, X
          DX = DBLE(X)
          SP = EXP(X)
          DP = EXP(DX)
          PDIFF = ABS(DP - DBLE(SP))/DBLE(SP)*100.00
          PRINT 5, PDIFF
        5 FORMAT (1X,'PERCENT DIFFERENCE = ',F8.4)
*
          END
*-----------------------------------------------------------*
```

6.
```
*-----------------------------------------------------------*
          LOGICAL FUNCTION  DIAG(ARRAY)
*
*  This function checks to see if the matrix is a diagonal matrix.
*
          REAL  ARRAY(4,4), SUM, DIAGON
          INTEGER  I, J
*
          SUM = 0.0
          DIAGON = 0.0
*
          DO 10 I = 1,4
             DIAGON = DIAGON + ABS (ARRAY(I,I))
             DO 5 J = 1,4
                SUM = SUM + ABS (ARRAY(I,J))
        5    CONTINUE
       10 CONTINUE
*
          IF ((SUM - DIAGON).EQ.0.0) THEN
             DIAG = .TRUE.
          ELSE
             DIAG = .FALSE.
          ENDIF
*
          RETURN
```

```
            END

      *------------------------------------------------------*
7.    *------------------------------------------------------*
            REAL FUNCTION   TRACE(ARRAY)
      *
      *  This function sums the values on the diagonal.
      *
            REAL  ARRAY(4,4)
            INTEGER  I
      *
            TRACE = 0.0
            DO 5 I = 1,4
                TRACE = TRACE + ARRAY(I,I)
          5 CONTINUE
      *
            RETURN
            END
      *------------------------------------------------------*

8.    *------------------------------------------------------*
            SUBROUTINE   TRANS (A, T)
      *
      *  This subroutine transposes array A to array T.
      *
            REAL  A(3,4), T(4,3)
            INTEGER  I, J
      *
            DO 10 I = 1,3
                DO 5 J = 1,4
                    T(J,I) = A(I,J)
          5     CONTINUE
         10 CONTINUE
      *
            RETURN
            END
      *------------------------------------------------------*

9.    *------------------------------------------------------*
            LOGICAL FUNCTION   UPPER(K,N)
      *
      *  This function returns a true value if K is
      *  an upper triangular matrix.
      *
            INTEGER  K(N,N), I, J
      *
            UPPER = .TRUE.
            DO 10 I=2,N
                DO 5 J=1,I-1
                    IF (K(I,J).NE.0) UPPER = .FALSE.
          5     CONTINUE
         10 CONTINUE
      *
            RETURN
```

```
          END


   *------------------------------------------------------------*

10.  *------------------------------------------------------------*
          LOGICAL FUNCTION   LOWER(K,N)
     *
     *  This function returns a true value if K is
     *  a lower triangular matrix.
     *
          INTEGER   K(N,N), I, J
     *
          LOWER = .TRUE.
          DO 10 I=1,N-1
             DO 5 J=I+1,N
                IF (K(I,J).NE.0) LOWER = .FALSE.
      5      CONTINUE
     10 CONTINUE
     *
          RETURN
          END
   *------------------------------------------------------------*
```

FORTRAN 77 EXAM - MIDTERM A

Problem 1	10 points
Problem 2	10 points
Problem 3	15 points
Problem 4	30 points
Problem 5	35 points

Total	100 points

1. What is the output when the following set of statements are executed?

```
REAL  A, B, C
A = 5.0
B = 5.5
C = 4.5
IF (A.GT.B) THEN
    PRINT*, 'FIRST'
ELSEIF (A.GT.C) THEN
    PRINT*, 'SECOND'
ELSEIF (B.GT.A) THEN
    PRINT*, 'THIRD'
ELSE
    PRINT*, 'FOURTH'
ENDIF
```

2. What is the value of COUNT after the following statements are executed?

```
INTEGER  COUNT, I, J
COUNT = 0
J = 2
DO 10 I=5,25,4+J
    COUNT = COUNT - 2
10 CONTINUE
```

3. Show the values stored in the array M after the following statements are executed:

```
INTEGER  M(0:9), I
DATA  M/10*4/
M(2) = 5
DO 10 I=1,10,2
    IF (I.LE.4) M(I) = -3
    M(I) = 2
10 CONTINUE
```

M

190

4. The equation below computes the distance between two points
   with coordinates (X1,Y1) and (X2,Y2).

$$\sqrt{(X1 - X2)^2 + (Y1 - Y2)^2}$$

Assume that values representing the coordinates of three
points have been stored in real variables X1,Y1,X2,Y2,X3,Y3.
Compute the area of the triangle formed by these three points
using the following equations, where A, B, and C represent
the sides of the triangle:

$$area = \sqrt{s(s-A)(s-B)(s-C)}$$

where s is equal to half of the sum
of the three sides of the triangle

Show type statements for all variables that you use. Store
the area in a real variable AREA. This is not a complete
program; you are just to show how to compute the area of the
triangle.

5. Write a complete F77 program to read a set of temperature
   measurements in a data file EXPER1. Each data line in the
   file contains two temperatures that were taken at the same
   time from two different points in a large piece of
   instrumentation. The last line in the data file contains
   values 999. and 999. Your program should compute the average
   temperature at the two points in the piece of
   instrumentation. A sample data file and the desired output
   format is shown below:

Data file: 70.   73.
             69.   70.
             73.   72.
             65.   65.
             999. 999.

Output format:

            AVERAGE VALUES
   TEMPERATURE 1   TEMPERATURE 2
      69.25   70.00.op

191

Solution to Midterm Exam A

1. SECOND

2. -8

3. 4   2   5   2   4   2   4   2   4   2

4.
```
REAL  X1,Y1,X2,Y2,X3,Y3,S12,S23,S13,S,AREA
  .
  .
  .
S12 = SQRT((X1 - X2)**2 + (Y1 - Y2)**2)
S13 = SQRT((X1 - X3)**2 + (Y1 - Y3)**2)
S23 = SQRT((X2 - X3)**2 + (Y2 - Y3)**2)
S = 0.5*(S12 + S13 + S23)
AREA = SQRT(S*(S - S12)*(S - S13)*(S - S23))
```

5.
```
*------------------------------------------------------------*
      PROGRAM  TEMPAV
*
* This program determines the average temperature
* from two locations in a piece of instrumentation.
*
      REAL  TEMP1,TEMP2,AVG1,AVG2,SUM1,SUM2
      INTEGER  COUNT
*
      OPEN (UNIT=2,FILE='EXPER1',STATUS='OLD')
*
      COUNT = 0
      SUM1 = 0.0
      SUM2 = 0.0
*
      READ (2,*) TEMP1, TEMP2
   10 IF ((TEMP1.NE.999.0).AND.(TEMP2.NE.999.0)) THEN
         COUNT = COUNT + 1
         SUM1 = SUM1 + TEMP1
         SUM2 = SUM2 + TEMP2
         READ (2,*) TEMP1, TEMP2
         GO TO 10
      ENDIF
*
      AVG1 = SUM1/REAL(COUNT)
      AVG2 = SUM2/REAL(COUNT)
      PRINT 20, AVG1, AVG2
   20 FORMAT (1X,10X,'AVERAGE VALUES'/1X,'TEMPERATURE 1',
     +         6X,'TEMPERATURE 2/1X,4X,F5.2,14X,F5.2)
*
      END
*------------------------------------------------------------*
```

NAME _____

FORTRAN 77 EXAM - MIDTERM B

Problem 1   10 points

Problem 2   15 points

Problem 3   20 points

Problem 4   20 points

Problem 5   35 points

Total   100 points

1. Give the value stored in RESULT after the following statements have been executed:

```
INTEGER  X, Y, B, RESULT
REAL  Z
X = 3
Y = -2
B = 10
Z = 5.0/2.0
RESULT = X*Y-B/INT(Z)-Y
```

2. Assume that three integers have been stored in the integer variables I, J, K. Give the F77 statements to print the literal EQUAL if I = J = K. Otherwise, print the literal ASCENDING ORDER if I < J < K, or print the literal DESCENDING ORDER if I > J > K. If the variables I, J, K are not in ascending order or descending order, print the literal OUT OF ORDER. This is not a complete program; just give the statements that determine and print the proper literal. A structured answer is necessary for full credit.

3. Consider the following set of statements:

```
      INTEGER  COUNT1, COUNT2, K, J
      COUNT1 = 0
      COUNT2 = 0
      DO 10 K=5,14,4
         COUNT1 = COUNT1 + K
         DO 5 J=0,4
            COUNT2 = COUNT2 + COUNT1
    5    CONTINUE
   10 CONTINUE
```

Give the values stored in COUNT1 and COUNT2 after these statements are executed.

COUNT1 _____   COUNT2 _____

4. Consider the following statements:

```
      INTEGER  K(5,2), I, J
      DO 10 I=1,5
         DO 5 J=1,2
            K(I,J) = I*J*2
    5    CONTINUE
   10 CONTINUE
      PRINT*, 'DATA VALUES'
      PRINT 12, (K(I,2), I=1,3)
   12 FORMAT (1X,I6)
```

(a) Draw a diagram of K and show the contents of it. Make rows run horizontal and columns run vertical.

(b)   What exactly is printed on the terminal screen?

5. Write a complete program that will read a data file that contains a set of measurements, with one measurement per line. The data file is called DATA5. The measurements are positive real values, and the last line in the data file contains the value -9.9 to signal the end of the data. Determine and print the percentage of the measurements (excluding the trailer signal) that are values greater than 10.0, and print the value in the following form:

XXX.X PERCENT OF MEASUREMENTS ARE GREATER THAN 10.0

Solution to Midterm Exam B

1. -9

2.
```
IF (I.EQ.J.AND.J.EQ.K) THEN
    PRINT*, 'EQUAL'
ELSEIF (I.LE.J.AND.J.LE.K) THEN
    PRINT*, 'ASCENDING ORDER'
ELSEIF (I.GE.J.AND.J.GE.K) THEN
    PRINT*, 'DESCENDING ORDER'
ELSE
    PRINT*, 'OUT OF ORDER'
ENDIF
```

3. COUNT1 = 27, COUNT2 = -230

4. (a) array K   2   4
                    4   8
                    6   12
                    8   16
                   10   20

    (b) DATA VALUES
                  4
                  8
                 12

5.
```
*-----------------------------------------------------------*
      PROGRAM   TEMPAV
*
* This program determines the average temperature
* from two locations in a piece of instrumentation.
*
      REAL   TEMP1
      INTEGER  COUNT, CT10
*
      OPEN (UNIT=2,FILE='DATA5',STATUS='OLD')
*
      COUNT = 0
      CT10 = 0
*
      READ (2,*) TEMP1
   10 IF (TEMP1.NE.-9.9) THEN
         COUNT = COUNT + 1
         IF (TEMP1.GT.10.0) CT10 = CT10 + 1
         READ (2,*) TEMP1
         GO TO 10
      ENDIF
      PRINT 20, REAL(CT10)/REAL(COUNT)*100.0
   20 FORMAT (1X,F5.1,'/1X,' PERCENT OF MEASUREMENTS ARE '
     +          'GREATER THAN 10.0')
*
      END
```

Name _____

FORTRAN 77 EXAM - FINAL A

Problems 1-7 (10 points each)	70 points
Problem 8	30 points
	_____
Total	100 points

1. What is the value of COUNT after executing the following statements:

```
         J = 1
         COUNT = 0
         DO 10 I=-5,5+J
           COUNT = COUNT + 1
      10 CONTINUE
```

Answer:_____

2. How many lines in a data file are read with the following loop?

```
         N = 1
      5  IF (N.LE.10) THEN
           READ (10,*) X
           N = N + 1
           GO TO 5
         ENDIF
```

Answer:_____

3. What value is stored in K(3) after the following statements are executed:

```
         INTEGER  K(10)
         DO 10 I=1,10
           K(I)  = 20 - I
      10 CONTINUE
```

Answer:_____

4. How many values are printed per output line in the following:

```
         PRINT 3, (X(I),I=1,10)
      3 FORMAT (1X,2F10.2)
```

Answer:_____

5. What is stored in the variable NAME after these statements
    are executed:

```
CHARACTER  NAME*10
NAME = 'T J SMITH'
DO 5 I=1,10
    IF (NAME(I:I).EQ.' ') NAME(I:I) = '.'
5 CONTINUE
```

                        Answer:_____

6. What is printed by the following statements?

```
REAL  X,Y
LOGICAL  OVER, DONE
X = 15.3
Y = 51.0
IF (X.GT.50.0) THEN
    OVER = .TRUE.
ELSE
    OVER = .FALSE.
ENDIF
IF (Y.LT.0.0) THEN
    OUT = .FALSE.
ELSE
    OUT = .TRUE.
ENDIF
IF (OVER.AND.OUT) THEN
    PRINT *, 'DONE'
ELSE
    PRINT *, 'NOT DONE'
ENDIF
```

                        Answer:_____

7. What is stored in X after the following statements are executed:

```
X = NUM(3.0,0.1,5)
.
.
.
END
REAL FUNCTION  NUM(A,B,F)
INTEGER F
REAL  A,B
NUM = A/B*2.0 + REAL(F)
RETURN
END
```

Answer:_____

8. Write a complete program that will read a STOCK data file and create a SALES data file. The STOCK data file contains information about items stored in a warehouse. Each line of the data file contains three values separated by blanks:

ID   identification number of the item (integer)
QUAN   quantity of the item in warehouse (integer)
PRICE   price of a single item (real)

You do not know how many lines are in the data file, and there is no trailer record at the end of the data file. You are to read the information in the STOCK file and create another file SALES which contains the same information but with a sales price instead of the regular price. The sales price is computed as shown below:

if regular price < $25.00, sale price is 10% off the
                    regular price
if regular price is between $25.00 and $100.00, including
     $25. and $100., sale price is 15% off regular price
if regular price is over $100.00, sale price is
     20% off regular price
          (example: regular price $20., then sales price $18.)

200

Solution to Final Exam A

1. 12.0

2. 10

3. 17

4. 2

5. T.J.SMITH.

6. NOT DONE

7. 7.0

8.
```
*----------------------------------------------------------------*
      PROGRAM  SALES
*
*  This program creates a data file with sale prices in it.
*
      INTEGER  ID, QUAN
      REAL   PRICE
*
      OPEN (UNIT=10,FILE='STOCK',STATUS='OLD')
      OPEN (UNIT=11,FILE='SALES',STATUS='NEW')
*
    5 READ (10,*,END=50) ID, QUAN, PRICE
         IF (PRICE.LT.25.0) THEN
            SALEPR = 0.9*PRICE
         ELSEIF (PRICE.LT.100.0) THEN
            SALEPR = 0.85*PRICE
         ELSE
            SALEPR = 0.80*PRICE
         ENDIF
         WRITE (11,*) ID, QUAN, SALEPR
         GO TO 5
   50 END
*----------------------------------------------------------------*
```

Name _____

FORTRAN 77 EXAM - FINAL B

Problems 1-7   70 points
(10 points each)

Problem 8   30 points
                     _____

Total   100 points

1. What is printed in an F6.2 specification if the output value is -3.8625? (Be sure to show blanks in the appropriate places if there are any.)

Answer:_____

2. What value is stored in Y after the following statements are executed:

```
REAL  X,A,Y
X = 3.0
A = 2.0
Y = X+3.0/A*5.0
```

Answer:_____

3. What value is stored in SUM after the following statements are executed:

```
INTEGER  N(5,3), SUM
DATA  N /10*1,5*3/
SUM = N(2,1) + N(2,2) + N(2,3)
```

Answer:_____

4. How many values are printed per output line in the following:

```
      DO 5 I=2,10,3
         PRINT 3, X(I)
3        FORMAT (1X,2F10.2)
5 CONTINUE
```

Answer:_____

5. What is stored in SUM after the following statements are executed:

```
SUM = 0
DO 10 I=1,25
    IF (MOD(I,7).EQ.0) SUM = SUM + I
10 CONTINUE
```

Answer:_____

6. What is stored in MZ after the following statements are executed:

```
REAL  Z(100,5), MZ
DO 10 I=1,100
    DO 5 J=1,5
        Z(I,J) = REAL(I+J)
5       CONTINUE
10  CONTINUE
    MZ = Z(3,1)
    DO 15 J=2,5
        IF (MZ.GT.Z(3,J)) MZ = Z(3,J)
15  CONTINUE
```

Answer:_____

7. What is printed   after the following statements are executed?

```
INTEGER  K(20)
DATA  K /20*0/
CALL SUBROUTINE  CHNG(K,5)
PRINT *, K(15)
END
SUBROUTINE  CHNG(K,N)
INTEGER  K(20), N
DO 10 I=N,20
    K(I) = I
10 CONTINUE
RETURN
END
```

Answer:_____

8. Write a subroutine called STAT which receives an array X of 100 real values that represent experimental test results taken at different times during an experiment. The experimental results will always be values greater than or equal to zero. The subroutine also receives another array PTR of 100 integer values that specify or point out which of the experimental results in the first array we are interested in. That is, if the first position of the integer array contains 1, then we are interested in the first experimental value; if the first position of the integer array contains 0, then we are not interested in the first experimental value. Therefore, if we are interested in all the experimental values, then the corresponding integer array will contain all 1's. If we are interested only in the last 10 experimental values, then the corresponding integer array will contain 90 zeros followed by ten 1's. If we are interested only in every other experimental value, then the corresponding integer array will contain alternating values of 1 and 0. The subroutine should then find and print the average AVE and the maximum value MAX using only the data in which we are interested. The calling statement is the following:

CALL STAT(X,PTR)

The output should be in the following format:

```
NUMBER OF VALUES USED IN COMPUTATIONS = XXX
AVERAGE = XXXX.XX
MAXIMUM = XXXX.XX
```

Solutions to Final Exam B

1. b-3.86

2. 10.5

3. 5

4. 1

5. 42

6. 8.0

7. 15

8.
```
*--------------------------------------------------------------*
      SUBROUTINE  STAT(X,PTR)
*
*  This subroutine computes the average and minimum value
*  from a a set of specified values in an array.
*
      REAL  X(100), XMAX, XSUM
      INTEGER  PTR(100), XCT, I
*
      XMAX = -1.0
      XSUM = 0.0
      XCT = 0
      DO 10 I=1,100
         IF (PTR(I).EQ.1) THEN
            XCT = XCT + 1
            XSUM = XSUM + X(I)
            IF (XMAX.LT.X(I)) XMAX = X(I)
         ENDIF
   10 CONTINUE
      PRINT 20, COUNT, XSUM/REAL(XCT), XMAX
   20 FORMAT (1X,'NUMBER OF VALUES USED IN COMPUTATIONS = ',
              I3/1X,'AVERAGE = ,F7.2/1X,'MAXIMUM = ',F7.2)
*
      END
*--------------------------------------------------------------*
```